College Freshmen Speak Out

College Freshmen Speak Out

Prepared by AGATHA TOWNSEND *for the Committee*
on School and College Relations of the Educational Records
Bureau

Foreword by BURTON P. FOWLER

HARPER & BROTHERS   PUBLISHERS   NEW YORK

COLLEGE FRESHMEN SPEAK OUT

Library of Congress catalog card number: 56-11920

Contents

58576

Foreword

BY BURTON P. FOWLER
Consultant, Fund for the Advancement of Education

A college campus is one of the most artificial communities in the world. It has its own peculiar form of group living. For centuries it has lacked the basic requirement of a natural society, that is, *diversity*. Representative of one age group, often of one sex, and of one kind of interests, these citizens of an unreal world have found escape either through the individualism of the classroom or the irresponsible immaturities of campus life. Rarely, but often enough to catch a glimpse of what a unified college society might become, one finds here and there experiments in a partial integration of classroom learning and mature campus living.

The one group in the college community which could contribute diversity, and thereby create some semblance of normality, tends to stand aloof except in the intellectual chaperonage of the classroom. Too often the faculty do not regard themselves as responsible citizens of this community in which they earn their living, thus depriving it of the ingredient so essential to mature, educative group living.

We speak glibly of bridging the gap as the number one problem of transition from high school to college. This gap, however, is not merely an intellectual jump that the high school senior makes from June to September. The testimony of the 470 freshmen in this book is more discerning. They discover, after they have safely landed on the college side, the same old academic road to be traveled before the new vistas are reached. As one freshman remarks "To my surprise, I found myself taking the same four subjects I had in high school. I was put in a French class where I read *Colomba* again for the third time."

The real gap between school and college, moreover, is not intellectual but emotional. At present we know much more about preparing students' minds for college than we do about their emotions. In dealing with the latter we have neither a curriculum nor dependable tests. This book is a story told by the freshmen themselves about their struggle for adjustment to a new world, a struggle for which their high school teachers, counselors, and parents had not fully prepared them.

The 20 per cent of these 470 freshmen who found their first year of college an unsatisfactory experience becomes 50 per cent if extended to a national basis. Such appalling wastage, regardless of the causes, suggests a need not only for a frank and fearless appraisal but for revolutionary changes in the curriculum and campus customs. No longer should the former be unrelated to student interests, nor the latter comprise a miscellany of cultural fragments and childish trivia.

The outspoken comments of this representative group of students from twenty-seven colleges reveal an amazing combination of approval and disapproval of their college experience, one of delight and despair, of too little freedom in some areas and too much in others. They indict an uncertain philosophy of the role of guidance in both school and in college. Too many of these eager, earnest young people sought vainly a pattern of purposeful values which they hoped to find in college experiences. "What

am I here for? What is a liberal arts education supposed to fit
you for? Am I another victim of the 'grand illusion'?"

There is little doubt that the present leap across the bridgeless
gap between school and college is for many freshmen a thrilling
and undisturbing adventure. These are the confident, mature,
well-prepared students. They are so able intellectually and so
stable emotionally that the multiplicity of adjustments does not
faze them. But there should be more to a liberal education than
being able to achieve a doubtful stability. One has a right to
question whether even this gifted group is getting a really liberal
education in terms of making the most of opportunities for non-
existent social responsibilities.

For a smaller but significantly large group, the freshman year
is fraught with shattering anxieties. And for all, the first year of
college—with its maze of roommates, new friendships, liquor,
sex, hazing, parties, athletics, fraternity rushing, adjustment to
new and impersonal ways of teaching, disturbed values, childish
campus customs, and lack of opportunities for unselfish service—
presents a challenge to the role of a liberal arts education which
college administrators can no longer ignore.

Why did these freshmen come to college? That is the $8000
question.

The liberal arts were designed to be instruments of culture,
that is, to uplift, inspire, serve and improve society; to kindle
enthusiasm for learning, so that men and women who enjoy such
a privilege will strive for the highest possible realization of fine
human relationships. Students so equipped will disdain college
riots, shoddy moral standards, selfish forms of motivation, and
discriminatory practices which hurt others. Classroom learning
and campus living will someday be so integrated that the college
community will no longer be an artificial but a real society, for
it will be concerned with the realities of community manage-
ment, the students and faculty together.

This book raises more questions than it answers. It provides no recipes for running a college or a high school. But for him who can read the signs, the road to a better quality of liberal education is well marked out.

College Freshmen Speak Out

How the Freshmen Told Their Story

I

COLLEGE freshmen may be homesick; uncertain of the reception they will have in their own class or among those mysterious figures of sophistication, the upperclassmen; troubled with doubts about their ability to meet the academic standards. They may blame their plight on their secondary schools, on their own intellectual equipment, or on college teaching methods or instructors. Often they do not know where to turn for help—to advisers appointed by the college, to their roommates, to faculty members, or to friends and counselors back home. Sometimes all of these resources seem to be a forlorn hope, and the freshman finds himself wondering "who cares?"

Obviously, many people are in fact interested in seeing freshman students make an effective adjustment to college. A high school principal said not long ago, "Our aim in college preparation is not to get our graduates admitted to the colleges of their choice, but to have them *succeed* in these colleges. Unfortunately, we rarely know how they are doing unless they are in serious trouble. We need better ways of learning about the later adjustment of our students—their social and personal success as well as their course grades." Another secondary school counselor

1

complained, "It has seemed to me that with all the questions asked by college admission counselors concerning the prospective college student they could in turn be just as eager to reciprocate with the same kind of evaluation as expected of the high school."

Colleges also rejoice in the successful student and are disturbed when their selection procedures have been carefully applied only to result in a freshman class which may be reduced to half its size after academic failure and voluntary withdrawal have taken their toll. Those students who continue in college as well as those who leave may be educational casualties. Almost any college would be anxious to learn a lesson from the freshman who said, "I know I have to have a college degree to succeed in the line of work I have chosen. But, believe me, that is the only reason I'm staying. The attitude of both faculty and students—neither of whom care a hoot—has completely disillusioned me." One college dean talks soberly about the responsibilities assumed by the college: ". . . having invested time, money, interest, and energy in the students who come, it is important to make the most of the abilities for success they have, and work at decreasing their liabilities, as part of the educational process. This seems sensible to us, and for this reason we work very hard with our freshmen, selecting our most appropriate teachers to teach them, and naming as freshman advisers the men and women most interested in this particular aspect of education. We rarely drop a student at the end of the first year, on the assumption that there is much human, educational, and social waste in doing so, and that educating a student to make the most of her capacities is worth a little time."

Are they ready for college?

How well or how poorly college freshmen adjust is not an accident. The freshman carries with him the effects of his home and community, his school, and the selection policies of his college. His equipment includes his own personal qualities, what he has absorbed in academic preparation, and the information and attitude with which he faces college. Any part of this equipment, or all of it, may be excellent, or some of it may be ill-suited to the reality the student faces when his first year of college begins.

A central problem of secondary schools and colleges has always been to evaluate the student's readiness for college. Educational literature is full of studies made with this aim. A series covering nearly a quarter century of college admission theories and practices has been issued by the Committee on School and College Relations of the Educational Records Bureau.[1] This series has striven to promote the articulation of school and college so that the whole educational process might have coherence and integrity for the individual student. Such studies help to improve communications between the two levels of educational institution and progress has in fact been made in bringing each into closer understanding with the other.

Even if the purposes of the college are better known to the schools, and vice versa, this does not mean that students are adequately prepared to live and work in college, and that colleges are ready to take up the educational sponsorship of the student with little dislocation. The fact that many who enter do not stay to complete their college courses, that transferring from one college to another is common, and that much of this loss occurs during or immediately after the freshman year suggests that the situation is far from perfect. Student drop-out and student transfer can be observed easily, and the figures indicate the extent to which the problems of going to college are still unsolved. The

[1] The latest in this series was: Arthur E. Traxler and Agatha Townsend, *Improving Transition from School to College* (New York: Harper & Brothers, 1953).

figures do not, however, tell *why* the problems remain or which are causing greatest difficulty.

The college freshmen speak

With the belief that their earlier studies gave adequate background in the policies and procedures of college admission, the Committee on School and College Relations determined that a new method of attack would shift attention from the institution to the person and attempt to draw upon what the college freshman actually experiences.

II

Asking people questions

Writing a letter to an unknown freshman, the committee was faced with the problem of asking for help in a special way. "Help us so that later classes will have a better time of it," was the essence of the appeal that accompanied a list of questions.[2] "Talk to us on paper, so that we can understand you better." The freshman was asked about academic matters—naturally. How easy was it to go from the classes and instruction of his high school to his college? Was the teaching as good in one place as the other? What was his motivation for study? Was he helped or handicapped by some particular aspect of his school preparation?

Another set of questions might well have been titled, "Managing New Experiences." It asked, in effect, "How do you get along now that you are on your own? How do you make out with new friends, roommates, finances, time schedules?" Other questions dealt with the social aspects of college life including organized activities or groups like fraternities, athletics, and so forth. The freshman was also asked about his attitudes toward other

[2] The questionnaire used is reproduced in Appendix A.

significant nonacademic features of college, as suggested by the terms "moral values, social values, relationship between sexes." The student was next asked to view his college, high school, and home as sources of help or as factors involved in his adjustment; and final questions dealt primarily with the college as it met and educated the student, and invited suggestions of ways that provisions for freshmen could be improved.

This is their own story

Asking people questions is a difficult and risky business. The committee was aware that the nature of the testimony from any freshman would depend on the questions asked and on the tone or mind-set established by the questionnaire as a whole. The main purpose of approaching the freshman at all was to persuade him to talk freely about his own experience. For this purpose, it was vital that the questions should be relatively "nonstructured," as the psychologist says—that is, the questions should in no way suggest that there were any "right answers," nor should they restrict the student so that he would omit or eliminate from consideration problems of any kind because of a feeling that they were not germane to the inquiry. In order to assure the student that he could be quite frank, the responses were kept anonymous.

The committee and the staff of the Educational Records Bureau, which handled the distribution and analysis of the questionnaires, recognized the unusual characteristics of the study. The freshman's own evaluation of his problems had to be accepted. If, because of the immediate events surrounding his response, he exaggerated the importance of one phase of his adjustment and neglected another, no external criterion could be applied to correct the picture he had given. Or if he felt some reticence at discussing some problem, he might give a false impression that it was unimportant. Moreover, even if one individual seemed to be "typical" of a whole group in his general responses, he represented, in the final analysis, no one but himself. Additive measures applied with too much enthusiasm, that is, too much "nose-counting" in the analysis of replies, might be full of error just because of the subjective, personal element in the responses.

The real interpretation of what the freshmen said must be left to the reader. This report includes, however, one piece of additional information which is important in rounding out the picture. This information consists of selections from the statements made by the dean or other faculty member at the college attended by the students. Drawing on his own experience with new students, he described those areas of adjustment which seemed of particular importance at his college. Frequently the college faculty members gave illuminating discussions of new practices or policies adopted by their colleges in an effort to aid freshmen in meeting the demands of their new life. Like the freshmen, the faculty commented on nonacademic as well as on scholastic affairs. The vividness of some of the statements fully equaled that of the student responses. Much of the significance of what the freshmen had to say is made clearer by these revelations of the attitudes and policies of those guiding the students. As later chapters will show, students and faculty sometimes hold different aims and expectations about the nature of college, and major problems occur if the two points of view are not reconciled.

III

The colleges take part in the study

When a college is asked to let its freshmen criticize, to open the doors to praise or blame, to hear about difficulties and dissatisfactions, to watch the process as some students go under because of their problems and hear others report growth and increased maturity, what is the reaction of the college? To judge from the colleges and universities approached in this study, the typical response is one of immediate interest, and a hope readily expressed that better understanding of the orientation of freshmen will result.

The four-year college members of the Educational Records Bureau and the other institutions of college level having a faculty member on the committee were invited to participate in the distribution of the final form of the questionnaire. Twenty-seven colleges were able to fit the undertaking into their schedules for the spring of 1954.[3] Like the students responding to the questionnaire, the colleges included were not necessarily representative of any group but themselves.

They were characterized only through their association with the Bureau, which carried an implication of particular interest in modern measurement and guidance programs, but in other respects they included almost every type of institution of higher learning. They ranged in enrollment from a few hundred to several thousand. There were in the group both publicly supported and independent colleges, both secular and denominational. These colleges were scattered over a wide area of the United States, from the eastern seaboard to California, and from Vermont to Texas, although a large proportion of them were in the East. They included an agricultural and mechanical college, a state university, several municipal colleges, a considerable number of endowed liberal arts colleges, and a teacher training institution. In selection policies, they ranged from those legally obligated to admit any student meeting defined requirements of residence and previous schooling, to colleges which have elaborate entrance procedures taking into account personal characteristics, educational aims, and many other aspects of fitness for their programs. There were twelve coeducational colleges, eight women's colleges, and seven men's colleges.

[3] A list of the cooperating colleges is given in Appendix B.

IV

Who are these freshmen?

The freshmen replying to the questions numbered 470 in all. Of these, 261 were women and 209 were men. They were distributed in the twenty-seven participating colleges with about eighteen students from each institution.

Like most freshmen, these were young. About two-thirds of them were eighteen years old—the women averaging a little younger than the men. Most of them came directly to college after graduation from secondary school.

Most of the freshmen had prepared for college in public high schools, although about a third came from independent schools. They came from small schools as well as large, with the largest percentage—over a quarter of the total group—graduating in a secondary school class of fifty or less. But some large classes from large cities contributed to the group.

The family background of many of the freshmen was such as to encourage college attendance. More than three-quarters of the group came from homes where the father's occupation was in the professional or managerial category. But, especially in the co-educational colleges, which, of course, include most of the state and municipal colleges, there were students whose fathers were engaged in many other sorts of occupations. More than half the fathers and about 45 per cent of the mothers attended college. However, this generalization conceals some interesting variations in groups from different types of colleges. For the students in the coeducational colleges, the majority of parents had not attended college. For the students in the men's colleges, the majority of the fathers had attended college but the majority of the mothers had not. For the freshmen in women's colleges, about three-fourths of the fathers and more than half the mothers had attended college.

Does it help a student adjust to his own college if his mother or father went to college? One freshman thought not: "My parents can't understand that things have changed since they went to college. So far as I can tell, the 'exclusive club' atmosphere must have prevailed a generation ago. It's certainly not like that now." On the other hand, a boy coming from a small rural community said, "If my father and the minister hadn't gone to college, I never would have. Only two others in my class even tried to go on after high school, and I found it a lonely row to hoe."

Both fraternity and sorority members were represented among the freshmen. However, none of the colleges for women had sororities on campus so the sorority women were drawn entirely from coeducational colleges. Of the 250 students apparently attending colleges where fraternities and sororities exist, 139 were members and 111 were not. Fraternity membership did not affect residence for most of these freshmen; only ten of the men lived in fraternity houses.

Other details on residence while in college reveal that the group included a fairly large number of students, especially in the coeducational colleges, who lived at home while attending. Most of the students in the municipal colleges did so, of course. The overwhelming majority of other freshmen lived in dormitories. Going to college for almost all these students meant that adjusting to a roommate was one of the first tasks required.

These notes on who the freshmen were and how they lived give the bare bones of fact. One cannot picture any individual by taking those circumstances of school preparation, home background, and residence which are characteristic of "most freshmen." It does become clear, however, that among these freshmen were persons of all sorts, in different college environments. Previous education, family fortunes, reactions to fraternity or sorority membership, and perhaps a hundred other things all helped make each man and woman an individual. But they shared a common experience of great importance. They had just made a vital move from school pupil to college student. How had they succeeded?

ONE

The Impact of College

I

* WHAT is it like to be a freshman? That is the theme of this book. A college is an institution for teaching students; it is also a community of persons living, working, and playing together. Like all human ventures, it is imperfect. Its weaknesses are particularly serious, however, because when a student flunks out and has to leave—or when he dislikes what he finds and withdraws of his own accord—money, energy, and potential rewards are then lost. The student himself is the only one who can say where the college has failed for him, and where it has succeeded. Perhaps he *did* go to the wrong college. Perhaps the academic standards are too high for him, or the social life too regimented or too undisciplined, or he does not know where to get help, or the college has set up no method for giving him help. On the other hand, new intellectual horizons may have opened for him; he may have made friends to cherish all his life, he may have found college a rich experience. From the stories of the students, whether happy or disappointed, lessons can be drawn for the college, for the schools preparing future classes, and for this year's or next year's freshmen as well.

II

College is not high school

College does not wait for the freshman to settle down with his roommate, his table in the dining hall, or his corridor in the dormitory before making its peculiar demands upon him. A college is an "academic" world, and soon makes itself felt as such. The introductory period, when the freshman learns something about the physical location of dormitory, library and classrooms, and the personal resources he has in his advisers, may be short or prolonged; but when classes start he recognizes that he is faced with serious business.

Scheduling alone makes far-reaching new demands on the freshman. Most classes in high school meet every day. In college, as much as a week may separate the sessions of a particular course. Assignments are increased proportionately, and the student finds himself with the problem of planning to master a much larger segment of the term's work before the next lecture or discussion can tell him how profitably he has spent his time. "Budgeting time was a terrific problem," writes a boy in a large university. "I used to be an awful procrastinator, and when I thought I had several days to prepare an assignment, the temptation to leave it till the last minute was almost overwhelming."

How do freshmen behave when asked to face the complexities of a university library? One freshman girl gave her reaction: "This was the problem—to be able to find sources of the necessary information and also, from the many books and chapters, to be able to draw out important and pertinent data. . . . My high school failed in that the assignments were too definite." This comment on the length and comprehensive quality of the college assignment is typical. The students mention study-reading frequently as the main way of getting information; the average freshman feels himself to be in a primarily "bookish" world. Slow reading can add directly to the length of study time required. How to listen to a lecture or how to organize and remember material from a discussion or a laboratory experiment also present problems.

Reading is not enough. Study must be reported. Long term-papers are mentioned more frequently than almost any other part of the academic load placed on the freshman. The perfectionist has his troubles: "I find my main difficulty is speed and self-confidence. When it comes time to type the paper I start changing a phrase here and a phrase there until I'm completely disgusted. Learn to do things quickly and well! Don't spend time re-copying. That's junior high school stuff." Complaints about course papers center around the same two difficulties which appear in the problem of reading: mastery of technique and budgeting of time. A major need felt by freshmen about term examination time is "that old problem, sleep."

Can the high school anticipate these difficulties?

Freshman comments are directed at high school as well. For example, one girl states, "About eight of my high school classmates who went to other colleges have had the same trouble I did with my freshman English. The teacher admitted she didn't like grammar and we got by without it, but here in college it's demanded of us." Writing correctly is only part of the difficulty. A boy from a private preparatory school says, "I feel that every high school should strengthen its work in such things as vocabulary, ability to read well and express yourself in writing, complete knowledge of term paper writing, how to take long tests, etc. These aren't just needed in English, but in every freshman course."

There is evidence that previous experience with a "college-like" approach to a course is useful. One girl reports," The English course which I took in my senior year was most helpful. It consisted of long reading assignments and numerous writing assignments, as well as intelligent discussions. Also, it was required to write a major report, comparable to term papers here."

The college and the nature of the freshman course

The courses themselves involve basic matters that help determine the freshman's whole reaction to college work: what subjects are required, how and by whom they are taught, the quality of challenge that they offer.

Some freshmen do not realize ahead of time that the college itself has made fundamental decisions about their education. As a university dean asked, "Who reads college catalogs? Certainly not the incoming freshmen." Many college faculties have worked long and hard to establish the theory and framework of the freshman course, and also to describe them in the much-maligned catalogs. The results of these college decisions may appear simply in the form of requiring Freshman English or Math, or they may be expressed in a whole group of integrated courses in the arts and sciences which are designed to provide a common background for later specialization.

A basic ingredient in the program has been left out, however, if the plans are not made clear—if not "sold"—to the freshman himself. When the student does not expect the requirements, surprise and indignation sometimes result. "How would you like to enter college, hoping finally to select your future course of life, only to find you *have* to take Western Civilization, or some such subject?" The reaction of this freshman is in sharp contrast to that of another who feels he is a partner in the planning. He says, "I am in an experimental core curriculum here that cuts through many subjects, and I find it most stimulating. Our work includes discussion of how the curriculum can be expanded and improved in the future."

Does the college encourage enthusiasm?

Satisfactions, as well as difficulties, arise from the pursuit of learning. Student after student finds that there is value in any accomplishment if only because it is his own. Where motivation runs high, it is credited largely to the feeling that the college man or woman does not *have* to be there, that he studies of his own free will, and that his standards are self-imposed.

Many elements go to make up the challenge that college presents to the mind of a freshman. The attitude of classmates, the nature of the courses, or the interest of an instructor may be the deciding factor. A girl in an eastern college for women is enthusiastic: "One of the striking differences between high school and college is the excitement and intense interest in study which is characteristic of this college." A boy describes the same kind of experience: "College was a whole new intellectual world for me, and it seemed as if it was the first time my mind had been stimulated."

"Stimulation" may be a tribute to the teacher rather than the course. On the other hand, students are quick to resent the course if the instructor is not interested in his subject, is perfunctory in his manner, or "considers the student merely another project or work-quota assignment." The difference in atmosphere is summed up by one girl: "I have learned a lot from instructors who didn't have that 'go ahead and flunk out—it means just one less student' attitude. They gave us real incentive to work."

III

How to be part of the college

Each college has an atmosphere of its own, made up of such subtle attributes that the freshman needs time to recognize it. College catalogs like to stress that the campus is "a friendly place," and so it seems to some students. But others find it too hard to accept those classmates who differ fundamentally from them, or feel that the number of congenial students is too small, and for them the friendliness fails. What takes place in the realm of the freshman's social and personal life can be just as critical for his over-all adjustment as what occurs when he deals with the academic element.

A mature student speaks of the "natural uneasiness" of most people starting in. "He has thousands of questions running through his head, such as 'Did I pick the right college? How should I make friends? Will the other freshmen accept me?' At one time or another each man has his doubts and thinks he would rather be somewhere else or feels he is being left out." The emphasis on finding a group of one's own is typical, and, typically, the freshmen find that the process takes time and involves some delays. "Many of us," one girl says, "thought we would walk into college and there would be about 150 girls to choose your friends from. This is a false illusion. It takes time to meet these people, and if you try to force it the more trouble you'll have. This is an important thing that should be stressed in high school."

Life at college provides many channels—sports, clubs in areas of special interest, and informal groups—which the freshman can investigate on his own initiative. Since most energetic newcomers are anxious to "belong," in one way or another, some soon find they have undertaken too much and have to retrench. The student who has been active in many high school organizations often finds that scheduling his extracurricular time is as much of a problem as scheduling his study. There are many individual patterns of recreation; one student may complain that he never finds enough time for exercise, while another finds that training for team sports demands a special schedule of rest which interferes with his roommate. Activities with less formal requirements still make demands on time, and the student may soon need to compromise among his interests. In the process, however, he has met several groups and felt at home with some of them.

To some extent, clubs and teams bring together homogeneous groups. Many of the contacts which the freshman makes, however, are more or less random, depending on outside factors such as assignments to certain classes or location in a particular dormitory. A girl who has never lived with a contemporary in the close quarters of a room where they entertain, work, and sleep may find a friend at once. Another student may discover she is living with someone whose habits, attitudes, and interests are so different from her own that only an armed truce or an open break is a tolerable solution. A different sort of adjustment may occur if roommates are already friends coming from the same public or private school. Such friends may form the nucleus of a small group of kindred spirits which excludes the stranger. This existence in a sort of social island may slow up the process of meeting, clashing with, or adjusting to a more diverse group.

Few freshmen find any virtues in the extreme variety of hazing. But several comment favorably on the rivalry between freshmen and upperclassmen that leads the freshmen to feel themselves as a unit. Such unity can help the newcomers find they have more in common than they had first discovered.

Freshmen look at fraternities

In contrast to those groups which the student investigates on his own, and those into which he is more or less thrust by assignment, are those which select their own membership, the fraternities or sororities. Because the idea of selection implies the idea of rejection as well, there are few topics which arouse such contrasting feelings. Not only the nonjoiners are critical. A fraternity man who reports that he is well satisfied with his group nevertheless deplores the "division of an already small class into even smaller fragments." Emotion runs high if a freshman feels he has been excluded because of some element in his background such as his religious affiliation. Hasty joining sometimes causes later disappointment. One boy reports, "The college can't house all its students and has to depend on frats. Because of this the frats pledge students even before school starts, and this is bad because it forces a student to join before he's really seen all sides to the story." There is a feeling that on some campuses the societies have too much influence. "Unless you belong to a sorority you're no good. This gives the girl who can't afford one an inferiority complex."

When the fraternity system works at its best, it evidently goes far to give the freshman a sense of security. The freshman takes personal and even academic troubles to a fraternity "brother" nearly as often as he takes them to the college adviser or counselor. The "house" shelters him, directs him, and may even dominate him, but above all it takes him in and gives him a feeling of belonging.

Independence and its responsibilities

All this discussion of the college men and women seeking out groups to join emphasizes the social being in each of them. They may feel, however, that personal satisfaction comes chiefly from an accent on individuality. "Being on my own was a wonderful feeling. Sure, I goofed plenty of times, but I like making my own mistakes, and when I really accomplish something I feel like it's all mine, too." Meeting new people, knowing those who differ as well as those who agree, sometimes leads an individual to a self-examination that produces a new awareness of his own standards. "We have some terrific bull sessions, because my roommate and I disagree on almost every conceivable topic. Of course I think he's wrong, but I never could understand before why anybody could feel like that." Tolerance, if not acceptance, is stressed by another boy: "The conflicting values of different people and groups bother very few. It is generally accepted that there should be all types of opinions and no one claims only one to be correct."

Positive statements about the values and conduct of their classmates come from several: "Morals are average, as I think you will find in any college. They are above those of people of our age who are not attending college." In contrast to the rigid supervision of school days is the freedom observed by one boy in an urban university: "The moral values here are very quiet, and very well observed. Individuals are a lot more responsible than in high school. I believe that is true not only because of maturity but because where a lot of snooping after the individual was done in school, here he is left entirely on his own."

Not all colleges provide this atmosphere of freedom, nor would all freshmen thrive on it if it were provided. There is some demand for even more control on the part of the college. Some students are profoundly disillusioned by laxity in social conduct on the campus. As one says, "Too many are just here for a free ride on papa's money. They have no responsibility toward their work or toward anything else. Drunkenness and worse are common." Another says, "Moral values? In a word, putrid." Is there no agreement at all from one college to another or from one person to another? Only, perhaps, in the fact that so many freshmen show deep concern with building their own concepts of worth and their own standards. No one is neutral when it comes to his own decisions.

The picture changes constantly and the pattern is frequently hard to see. Even before any attempt is made at systematic interpretation, the facts of contrast and conflict thrust themselves up for attention. Freshmen come with background and training that are almost incredibly far apart until one reflects on the different sorts of towns, homes, and schools that exist in this country. And colleges differ almost as radically.

IV

Guidance into college

Being a freshman is an emotional experience. Some of the emotions are negative, a response to confusion or frustration. The quotations already given illustrate the lack of full preparation with which the freshman faces college. There is striking repetition of such phrases as "I certainly was surprised," and "I had no idea." The aspects of life at college which annoy one person may be acceptable to another, but practically no one likes the "surprise factor" when it assumes the proportions of a rude awakening.

Perhaps the mistake is rooted in the past, even so far back as the initial consideration of a college to attend. There are many ways of selecting a college, and several freshmen point out that they used the wrong ones. "Don't see why people told me to go East to college. I'm sure there are good middlewestern colleges where I would have a better chance at an education." Most students are loyal to family preferences, but one does say, "A person should never be expected to succeed at a college just because his father went there." Another writes, "I didn't expect to go to college and didn't take the right courses. This looked like the only place I could get in, but I might better have taken another year to make up the work and gone somewhere else. Anywhere!"

Young men and women who seemed well adjusted in the schools they attended nevertheless may be critical because they should have had a better idea of what to expect. "I think there was too much emphasis on making high grades for college entrance, but not enough on other kinds of preparation. If only I could have talked to some of the graduates from [my high school] who went here I could have saved days of time in the beginning." "My headmaster went here to college, but he should have realized the place could change a lot in forty years."

This plea for recent, first-hand information from students

already at the college under consideration is frequently made. "We had College Night," writes one student, "and I got a good idea about the academic side, sports, and so on, but no college registrar could explain about the fraternity politics here." A number of freshmen have found that information on the academic side was better than enlightenment about other aspects of college. "Scholastically, this place is tops. But I had no idea that my activity would be so restricted. I was used to the freedom of a public high school, but here we are scarcely allowed off campus."

A high school may have a climate of competition, of domination by teachers, or on the other hand, of more personal attention and less stress than exists in some colleges. A student will not necessarily adjust best to a college that is like his high school, but one graduate says, "My high school should have prepared me for competition and large classes in college. We were encouraged to think for ourselves, and that is all very well. But, we weren't aggressive enough to speak up in a big group of people." Evaluation methods and marking differ. "I spent the whole first term wondering if I was doing what was expected. In a small high school class I could tell, but here I just felt like a very small fish in a stream."

These complaints come typically from graduates going from comparatively small high schools to larger institutions. On the other side is a plea from a boy prepared in a large city high school. "The biggest thing my school could do is to have some counselor who would get to know each student really well. I never had anyone who took a personal interest in my work who knew beans about higher education and could have told me how to get the most out of the courses offered at school. I could have had more science if I had known it would help, but it wasn't required and nobody suggested it would save me time here. Also, I think college prep kids would work better if somebody was interested in *them*, not just their marks."

The need for help remains

Freshmen echo this request for personal attention at the college level as well. "As for my adviser, I've only seen him twice, once to make out my schedule and once to change a course. He has about 75 freshmen and wouldn't know me from a hole in a wall." There is repeated praise for college instructors who make an effort to know their students, and surprised pleasure when they make time to meet groups informally outside of class. This praise is in contrast to notes like this: "The college does nothing to break down the completely impersonal approach used in freshman classes." And even a potentially good system of student counseling is ineffective if it hasn't been made real to the individual student. "I know there is supposed to be a good testing bureau and a staff of psychologists. I guess I've been too bogged down in my own problems to go and see them."

Freshmen do not wish to be coddled. Their requests and suggestions are for more information, given with friendly interest, both before and after they enter college. Their desire is for some relief from the mystery that surrounds adjustment to college, less surprise at academic and social requirements, and more help in their direct attack on the problems of learning and living at college. They are enthusiastic at finding new stimulation and acquiring knowledge. They share with high schools and colleges alike a great impatience with policies that seem to slow up adjustment, or conditions and practices that make this transition a difficult one.

TWO

School Plus College
Equals What?

COLLEGE adjustment does not begin with arrival on campus. Many of the initial difficulties faced by the freshman might have been avoided before the student entered college at all. What is the role of the high school in freshman adjustment?

Secondary schools have long been concerned with academic preparation. This function of the school is recognized by the students, and the instruction received in high school comes in for comment after the graduate tries out his equipment in his college courses. But preparation does not consist purely of classes and courses. There is, for example, the matter of college selection. "My high school did a good job academically," one student reports, "but a lousy job when the principal encouraged me to come *here* to college." A scholarship student complains, "I know now that I should have taken the smaller scholarship at [another college] because it didn't require so much work. Someone should have helped me realize that here my recreation time would be *nil.*" A boy who states that he is withdrawing from his college after the first year gives as his reason, "I was advised to come here because of low tuition costs. I didn't realize that I was neither equipped for or interested in a technical school."

Other freshmen agree that some of their most pressing difficulties go back to this problem of selection, that their high schools and the colleges could have helped more at the preliminary stages. Nearly a third of the group mentioning selection problems said that financial needs had created difficulties. Large numbers stated that they did not understand the relation of selecting a college to their vocational objectives or plans. Educational objectives were sometimes even hazier. "What is a liberal arts education supposed to fit you for?" asked one boy.

How do you find the right college?

Some students choose their colleges because they believe that only a certain group of institutions are within their reach economically. Some limit their choice to colleges in their home city or its immediate neighborhood, so they can live with their families. For others, the differential in costs between a state-supported college or university and an endowed college is the decisive factor. Supplementing funds from home by working at college is hard for the freshman. Preference in jobs is given to upperclassmen whose records are good, as colleges are naturally anxious to help such students complete their work. Scholarship aid is available for some beginning students, but competition is keen, and certain scholarship holders find that the obligation to maintain good work creates anxieties which make the tension of the first year even more pronounced.

Colleges are not satisfied that the students have been adequately helped to assess the economic facts. One dean states that "many students take the wrong approach. The clue to this problem is that applicants do not know of the money available at many colleges—money which can be given even to freshmen." Academic standing in high school and ability to do college work become of critical importance to the candidate who does not wish to have his choice of college dictated by cost alone. But achieving a high school standing worthy of scholarship aid is a long-range matter; it cannot be left until the student begins to send in application blanks.

Other considerations which determined the selection of colleges are less tangible than finances, but equally powerful. Some students—like the Minnesota boy who said he believed he "had to go East to college"—are influenced by "prestige." This factor has been defined by one college dean as "the grand illusion" in college selection. Certain high schools—public and private—develop a tradition of "sending students to the best colleges." How closely do the students, their parents, and their school counselors examine the meaning of "best" in the light of the needs and aspirations of the individual boy or girl? The fact that one's friends were going to a specific college, the fact that an older relative attended, or simply the fact that one read a magazine article describing a lovely campus have all led to mistakes.

Many difficulties could be avoided if high school students gave less attention to peripheral matters like finance and geography and more heed to educational programs. More than a third of the freshmen in men's colleges discussed their troubles in squaring their college courses with their scholastic and vocational aims. The women, too, tried to evaluate both the educational and the prevocational meaning of their college work. One girl said pointedly, "I still believe in liberal arts for women, because I believe I will be a better homemaker and a better member of the community with a well-rounded education. But I intend to work at a job, too, and wish I had more faith in the practical usefulness of a social science major."

"I don't think I know myself well enough," said one boy in a large university. "I want to explore my interests in college. But what I really wish I had is a better idea of my own abilities, and I feel strongly that my high school should have helped me more in this."

The secondary school has an opportunity to help the future freshman avoid difficulties by providing adequate data to the candidate about his school progress and his presumed strengths and weaknesses in ability, and by helping him crystallize his thinking about what he wants from his education. These data will not only help him select colleges for consideration but will also give him a more adequate idea of what to expect where he does go. The college, too, should be urged to give both the applicant and his school the most accurate possible picture of its requirements and its operation. Platitudes and attractive descriptions in the catalog are not enough.

Difficulty in selecting a college stems from lack of information —the candidate's lack of information about himself, and an equal lack of knowledge about the college. These two elements reappear once the student becomes a freshman in his college, contributing to his uncertainty and surprise. This alone should be enough to put the problem high on the list for colleges as well as secondary schools.

II

Evaluating the secondary school

Selecting a college and forming an adequate picture of what it will be like are only one part of preparing oneself for the experience. Supposedly, freshmen have been readying themselves for college *studies* for some time. Direct instruction is, after all, the unique function of both school and college. Secondary schools deplore excessive domination of the curriculum by college requirements. Colleges complain about the great differences in the standards of preparation apparent in the graduates from different schools. The freshmen may be little concerned with the philosophy of the relations between school and college, but they are deeply involved in the results.

How do freshmen feel about their previous schooling? A good percentage, nearly half of those replying, regarded their preparation as good or even excellent. Students say, "My high school certainly has earned its reputation for good preparatory work." Or, "When I compare myself with other freshmen, I realize I was fortunate." But those whose academic adjustment gives rise to problems are equally sweeping: "It doesn't seem as if *anything* I did in high school prepared me for this place!" For many young men and women, of course, a middle position seems more defensible; nearly a third of the freshmen stated that the secondary school had given them a good send-off in some courses and poor preparation in others.

Schools are not equally strong in all subject areas, and the freshmen find holes in their preparation. "I came from a school with a very poor science program," says one boy. Another, now struggling with an arts program, reports, "I guess what my high school lacked was 'cultural' preparation. References to literature that is perfectly familiar to my classmates are all Greek to me. We never had to read." Some graduates recognize that goals other than college entrance were set up for some courses, and that it may be difficult to give work that is meaningful both to those who expect to go on further in a subject and to those whose high school course is terminal. "Only three of my class went to college, so of course our work wasn't specially organized." Others blame themselves for difficulties in some subjects, implying that the school course might have been adequate but their own pattern of abilities made certain courses troublesome regardless of this background. Some ruefully say, "I should have been *made* to do better work in math [or languages or history . . .]."

Although there is no agreement that individual subjects are generally well or poorly taught, one area calls forth more comment than any other. This is the field of oral and written expression, and the other "communications skills" such as reading and listening to a lecture or discussion. The need for training in these techniques is either implied or stated in many of the complaints concerning the length and complexity of the college assignment.

Goals for high school English

It follows that the school's English course is more frequently mentioned than any other. Many students apparently feel that they did not take full advantage of what was offered and others maintain that additions to the typical course are needed. They point out that the English course should teach the student how to read, how to select and evaluate material, how to use a library, how to take notes, outline for a report or test, and above all how to make written reports in standard English without difficulties in spelling, usage, and the like. The two needs most clearly expressed are those for rapid reading and the ability to write grammatically.

Students with greater insight into the complexities of the tasks of reading realize that while merely "getting through" the extensive college reading assignment is a major problem for the slow reader, the more important need is for flexibility in reading skills: knowing where skimming is indicated, where careful reading and re-reading is required, how to seek evidence to solve a problem, how to compare and criticize sources. Some students appreciate more vividly than others the differences between the short written assignments common in school and the sustained effort needed to organize a term paper.

High school educators might question whether all of these skills are best placed in the English curriculum alone. The reading abilities needed for certain subjects may better be developed in the curricula of those subjects. There are clearly differences in the way of tackling reading for courses in history, journalism, and physics. Formal grammar is a study shared by the foreign language departments. Standard English expression, correct spelling, and the proof-reading of written work may be demanded in any subject. Moreover, the time available to the English curriculum is not unlimited, and other objectives of high school English— such as the development of sensitivity or appreciation in language, creative expression, and the world of literary acquaintance— cannot be abandoned if literate students are to be graduated. Nevertheless, the difficulty of rethinking present courses of study or standards of performance is no excuse for avoiding the task.

The deans agree

Independent support for the opinion of the freshmen comes from some of the college officers. The dean of a large coeducational college highlights difficulties in reading and writing as a serious problem:

The most acute inadequacies in study techniques are in reading competence, particularly where it is the task to prepare an assignment by using several books and by organizing the material gleaned therefrom. This requires ability in note-taking far removed from the habits of transcribing which the student is apt to bring from high school. Added to the note-taking there is often deficiency in expressing in simple, intelligible, expository form what one has learned from the readings. Perhaps the college teacher expects too much, but it would seem that high schools might well give more thought to developing these skills rather than over-emphasizing the content value for seniors who plan to go to college.

Special recognition of the need for something beyond border-line competence in writing is given by the dean of freshmen at a men's college. He says:

A few freshmen, by no means lacking in basic potentiality, tell me that they never wrote a theme until they came to college. . . . The difficulty does not, of course, have to do always, or solely, with matters of grammatical construction. Problems of style can be equally, if not more, baffling for a student who has done a bare minimum of writing in his entire life. It is not heartening, nor very enlightening, simply to tell a student that his paper is badly written, that it lacks tone and qualitative expression. This apparently calls for a level of sensitive perception that the average person can get only by reading and no little amount of practice in writing.

Long before entrance, freshmen have heard about the importance of verbal ability for success in college. This emphasis has appeared, for instance, in the types of entrance examinations required—both in verbal scores on tests of academic aptitude and in the administration of separate tests of English and reading. According to a previous study made of college entrance policies and procedures (summarized in *Improving Transition from School to College*[1]), English tests are more frequently used for admission and placement than tests in any other subject. Even after such selection, however, the range of standing in the verbal skills is so great that many students are handicapped in the usual college assignment.

III

The equipment of the student

Part of the task of the initial year in college is simply to survive. New demands come both from the teachers and students at college and from the individual himself as he sets new goals and purposes for his effort. But he faces these requirements with only a guess about his preparation. On what does he base his estimate that he is ready for college? He has learned facts and ideas, and has acquired attitudes, in high school courses. He has learned how to study, or at least he has formed a set of habits in tackling his work; these habits he regards as study methods. From his marks or grades he has built up notions about the adequacy of his knowledge and the effectiveness of his work habits. Both those learnings retained from his high school subjects and those study habits he has brought with him furnish the experience he tries to transfer to college work.

[1] Traxler and Townsend, *op. cit.*, p. 48.

Even though the freshmen identified many of their study difficulties with their English courses, a closer look suggests that problems arose in connection with a number of fields, and really meant that the novice was attacking advanced work with poor tools. Yet many of the young men and women showed genuine surprise that the tools were poor. In the colleges with selective entrance programs, the surprise was all the greater. The students had attained, as they knew, superior school records which had helped admit them to the very courses they now found most baffling. Why were their efforts to attain comparable standing in college meeting with so much frustration?

The nature of college work

Length of assignment and reading load is only part of the change from high school to college work. There is a change in complexity as well. Reading must be not only more extensive but more selective. Information given in one reference source must be checked, criticized, and perhaps rejected because of information given in another. The task of evaluation, in other words, assumes major significance.

In learning how to evaluate what is read, or observed in a laboratory experiment, or heard in a class discussion, the student finds his concept of the role of the teacher undergoing change. No longer, in most colleges, does the instructor check on detailed completion of assignments. As several freshmen put it, "The teacher isn't there looking over your shoulder to see that you do what you're told." What is the teacher doing? In general, his help and direction are given through lectures and discussion, from which the student must find his clues to the selecting, evaluating job that he is doing as his part of the course. Class notes assume new importance because they are needed for guidance in the reading and writing done later.

College examinations also serve purposes different from those of the high school test. "High school tests were mostly factual, the short-answer type. These college examinations where you have to think about the whole month's work, or more, are a terrific strain." The reason for the strain is expressed this way by one boy: "For the first time, now, I am trying to reach as deep into subject matter as possible and understand as much as possible." Because they take more time to give and correct, and because they are so much broader in scope, college examinations are relatively less frequent but correspondingly more important for class standing. These characteristics of the program, of course, make it increasingly urgent for the student to do his self-evaluating as accurately, and his work between tests as responsibly, as possible.

All these comments on changes in assignment and testing are significant because they underline differences not only in the studying but in the *thinking* required in college. The student who reports that "high school didn't teach me to think, only to learn facts," and the one who states that "the actual thought processes were practically completed for you," also refer to the difficulty of learning how to make generalizations, do abstract reasoning, and manipulate ideas without losing sight of their basis in experience. Facts are no longer presented to be learned merely because they exist but because of their relation to the thinking required in a course. Thus, in some science courses, a first-year student will report, "I was amazed that I actually had to memorize formulas and laws in order to do my work efficiently."

In this evidence that college work differs both in quantity and in kind from high school tasks there is an important comment on the general complaint that study methods which were previously effective are no longer bringing results. The students talk at length about their aims of study in college—to get into the heart of a subject, to relate what is learned to remote vocational plans, to become liberally educated, to learn how to think. If their analysis is correct, then they may be attempting to transfer study methods which are actually inappropriate and improper.

Getting the work done

Developing new habits and devising methods of approach to new problems are time-consuming. Yet most students feel that the new work load cannot wait, and a proportion of them know by bitter experience that "it is a cycle. At first I never seemed to get my work and sleeping both done. I got more and more tired and found myself less interested in my classes and my work took longer and longer." One such girl goes on to say, "The whole problem was budgeting time and knowing what is most important, what will take most time, and how to schedule from that." Even people of high capability are challenged and frustrated by the need to make new adjustments quickly.

More frequent mention was given to this problem of organization for attack than to any other source of academic difficulty. Recognizing that much effort goes into waste motion and that mistakes in estimating tasks are costly, a disconcerting number of freshmen, virtually a third of them, felt that they were unable to deal with it successfully.

There is a whole set of difficulties of which the inability to organize work and study is a symptom. When, for the sake of analysis, the students reporting were divided into categories regarded as either well or poorly adjusted, it was observed that nearly twice as many of the poorly adjusted group reported difficulties in scheduling and planning for study. "Poor adjustment" as defined for this analysis was not synonymous with academic failure. Poorly adjusted students had difficulties in the personal and social areas as well as problems in scholastic progress. But, this one aspect of *inability to organize* was characteristic of the whole group of students having marked trouble in college.

College standards

How hard it is to succeed academically in college can be known in the end only in terms of the individual, his ability, his preparation, his college, and his desire to succeed. Information that will give a good picture of any of these elements is at a premium. At the present time, college selection practices and placement testing give clues to general ability and preparation. But specific factors like the capacity for high level reasoning, familiarity with the tools of learning like reading efficiency and good study skills, motivation, and above all the ability to develop and apply new techniques—these require careful analysis.

College work undoubtedly *seems* difficult. The neophyte has to carry more courses, do longer assignments, and exercise a greater amount of self-direction than before. But how much of the difficulty is intrinsic in the demands made on the student and how much of it is a quality of the newness in the situation is hard to decide. If the freshman is tentative because he feels he does not know what is expected of him, he may increase his own burden by trying to do everything that might conceivably be desired. If he has trouble expressing himself fluently and correctly, he may conceal from his instructors what mastery he has attained. If his preparation has serious gaps, he may slight the courses which seem easier in order to try to make up for his weakness in others; as a result, he may find that he does poorly in his strongest subject.

Avoiding difficulties is more sensible than trying to remedy them after they have occurred. The freshmen speaking through this study do not all have sufficient understanding to describe either just what their problems in academic adjustment are or how they could have been avoided. As a group, however, they ask for help! College standards that are mysterious and ill-defined do not seem high; they seem merely unreasonable. The *real* standards—demands for clear thinking, for careful, sustained and thorough study, for broadening insights and quickening appreciations—should be brought forcibly to the attention of the students. These standards are difficult enough, but they are central to the problem of college education.

IV

The college plans the freshman year

The fourth quarter of the educational course is necessarily tied to and related to the three four-year periods that preceded it. True, it involves a change of scene and a new approach, but a certain amount of continuity is inevitable. The sixteen years of training are all aimed at the same individual. What, then, does going to college do to the *trend* of education?

This question emerges from the comments and questions, the complaints and disillusionments, of the young men and women who describe their freshman year. The college, it appears to these beginners, reigns in its own world, and operates autocratically. College faculties and administrations, either deliberately or through tradition and inertia, hold certain concepts of what the freshman year should be. These concepts range from a commitment to a uniform program which may cover almost all the two years of "lower division" work, to the acceptance of an elective program for all students, with course selections made wholly in the light of the student's own aims and desires. The first pattern, of entire or partial prescription, is by far the more usual one.

Required courses

It is the purpose of this study to describe the impact of college policy on the freshman, rather than to defend the policy. The colleges may draw such inferences as they wish from the students' own words. One inference is clear: the effects of prescription are negative, serious, and discouraging. When the students were asked to indicate the sources of their academic difficulties, selection of courses for which they had little interest ranked second, exceeded only by the proportion of students reporting poor work and study methods. Women in colleges for women, it is significant to note, checked lack of interest in first-year courses more frequently than any other item in the field of academic adjustment. Over all, for both men and women in colleges of all types, about one in four found the nature of freshman work dispiriting.

The mere fact of requirement goes hard with some people. The late adolescent is restive at prescription; even while he begins to recognize that choices are restricted all through life, his impulse to self-direction is strong. "Again here I find that I am forced to take courses in which I have absolutely no interest on the theory that they round out my education. While this didn't bother me in high school, I'm getting tired of wasting time on courses which do me no good." Claims that the college entrant is more mature than his advisers realize are frequent. "After all, if a person is old enough to decide whether or not he or she wants to come to college, the person is, more than likely, able to decide what he wants to become, and not have someone else tell him what to do."

First-year requirements vary from college to college, but there is striking similarity in the frequency with which the students react negatively to their restrictions. Even if the proportion of students distressed and discouraged by prescription of courses were much smaller than it is, this would remain a problem needing the attention of the college. Does the college itself know why the freshman course is set up the way it is? This should no longer be considered a professional secret.

Does the college trust the high school?

Requirements are especially onerous if they involve repetition of work done earlier. Even if, in theory, college is a continuation of previous instruction, some freshmen find that their first-year work backtracks on ground already covered. Loss of motivation and interest results if this work occupies more than a small part of the time. It is useless to point out to the boy who reports that college French has just forced him to read *Colomba* for the third time that language preparation varies greatly in high schools, and that a heterogeneous class has resulted. Boredom may infect all parts of his study.

"I imagined this would be a place of higher learning and more advanced study of what I had studied and mastered in high school. A number of others came with the same thoughts I did, only to be rudely awakened to the fact that what they did in high school seemed to have no bearing whatsoever on college." Another boy states, "Maybe I was too well prepared. I found all my courses except English repeat a lot of previous material. The transition didn't seem one of integration and continuous progress, but rather a regression." These two students had high averages in school but were not permitted by their colleges to enter advanced courses, in spite of recommendations for such a step from their former high school principals.

What are the freshmen saying? That colleges are allowing students to lose momentum and interest in learning because of the lack of imagination shown by the requirements or the way they are administered. Sound programs are missing fire because they are applied mechanically, with no relation to the student's previous education. Is there a connection between these generalizations and the fact that nearly half the freshmen entering college do not return for a second year? This is a question assigned by the students for their colleges.

v

How does the college teach?

The college makes many decisions regarding its freshmen in addition to those related to the pattern of courses. None are more critical than the decisions about the faculty members into whose hands this instruction is put. One freshman girl stated a truism when she pointed out that "I have some teachers who could make me interested in learning anything on earth. And I have two others who could take the heart and life out of the best course that ever was."

Fortunately, six out of ten freshmen believed that college teaching was better than the instruction they had in high school, or was at least as good. However, a sizable group, almost a fifth, reported that one of the sources of their difficulty was "questionable teaching ability of instructors." The teacher's apparent lack of interest in the subject matter was a frequent criticism. Other students, particularly those assigned to large classes, ascribed perfunctory attitudes to their lecturers and there were numerous complaints of instructors who were hard to approach.

Some association of teaching problems with the requirement of courses was made. "The student feels, and even *knows*, that the teacher is not concerned with whether he passes or fails. But you can't help feeling sorry for the poor guy because he knows the men are in there just because they are required to be, not because they want to take it."

Skillful teachers can apply a variety of methods for the presentation of subject matter. But certain instructors apparently fail to make the type of class organization in effect either palatable or justifiable to the freshmen. "During high school I was much more interested in my subjects because the students could take more part in the class work. I have some lecture classes here where there is no talk at all from the students." In such an instance, the significant fact is loss of motivation for study and for further pursuit of college work if the fear arises that advanced courses will bring a repetition of frustration.

The effect of uninspiring teaching in introductory courses can be serious for preparation needed for later work in major fields. This effect reaches even beyond the acquisition of basic skills and understanding. Good relationships between teachers and students play a central role in all functions of the college. College students make decisions influencing the whole trend of their intellectual lives as they select courses and academic activities. And persons as well as ideas go a long way to determine the students' concepts of the purposes and results of scholarship.

What kind of person comes to stand for the profession of biologist or mathematician or linguist? Does he reflect his own fascination and personal involvement with his work and teach as though it were vital for others to share his insights and enthusiasm? Does he recognize the real validity and importance of the beginning courses in his field? Perhaps most significant of all, can he make himself accessible to the freshman, not just to answer questions on class work but also to give the feeling that he and the student share in the challenge of his subject? The poor teacher can, because of inadequacies in his concept of his task as teacher or his lack of adjustment to the problems of the beginner in his field, present an unattractive sample of his profession.

Freshmen and freshman instructors

The responsibility assumed in teaching freshmen cannot be overemphasized. Yet it is often handed, as colleges admit, to less experienced instructors. The interest which older members of the faculty take in advanced work, and their greater concern with those students majoring in a field, are natural and understandable. It is hard to identify the future professional leader in a freshman class, and it may be hard to reconcile using the time and energy of the master teacher for the freshmen who may never go on to build upon the foundation laid. In other words, it takes thought and effort to decide on the nature and purpose of the freshman course for a mixed group. Compromises must be made between the need to give initial training to future specialists in the field and the desire to make the single course for those whose major interest will lie elsewhere a meaningful, broadening experience.

While the freshmen give plenty of indication that this matter of who teaches is crucial, there is almost no mention of the question in the statements from college officers. Yet this is a problem which the college alone can alleviate. Perhaps time will see more faculties pondering the objectives set for them by one dean who did recognize this difficulty. He states:

Looking at the over-all question of freshman adjustment on the academic level, I have developed a very strong conviction at one point, namely, that freshmen should have the highest quality teaching an institution can offer. This is the crucial time, in my judgment, for getting the intellectual imagination in operation and for giving the student the maximum opportunity for the satisfaction that comes with substantial achievement and a sense of developing competence in given areas. The teachers best equipped for doing this may, and will, include some of the younger faculty. On the whole, however, it seems to me unfortunate that some of the older, experienced, and most able members of a faculty should not be teaching at this crucial level. . . . In any event, it is my belief that a strong case can be made for exposing freshmen to the most sensitive, capable, and stimulating teaching a school can afford.

Selection of instructors and improvement of instruction is a frontier area for colleges. The comments of freshmen lend particular importance to the few experiments which have been started. It will be hard for the prospective student to find out what kind of teaching is done on various campuses unless he is told by students now enrolled. Admission officers, alert to the importance of the problem, should convince their colleagues of the strong selling point they would have if they could say, "Our best men teach the freshman courses. . . . You'll have a chance to work under one of the really distinguished minds in this field."

VI

Motives for work

As the freshman's academic year gets under way, the visitor to a campus sees the college in full swing. A schedule of classes is in effect. Teachers lecture, conduct discussions, supervise laboratories, advise on extracurricular activities, and perform a myriad other tasks. The library is open, the dormitories and fraternity houses also provide settings for study, and the freshman shuttles from one place to another at top speed, racing in an effort to keep up with his work. But at least one important part of the operation is concealed from view. This is the motivation behind the activity—the force which sends the student ahead in spite of a heavy load of studying, confusion in his adjustment to persons around him, and doubts about whether he is "making the grade." In short, as the student might put it himself, why does he stay in this rat race and what does he get out of it?

Both students and faculty know that motivation is a basic ingredient for the success of the whole process. The faculty has seen students of mediocre ability succeed because of good motivation. They have also seen brilliant students falter, rebel against college situations, and fail. As for the freshmen, one already recognizes that "I have learned to keep myself going even when a course is tough or uninteresting because it meets requirements I have laid down for myself." Another says, "Reasons for studying are the first and most important difference between school and college. . . . Now I can only put it that I am studying for personal and intellectual betterment." Others give other reasons, but there is an echo from student to student: "Now I study because I want to. Now I am really on my own. Now I set my own goals."

Fully half the freshmen talk about change in motivation when they discuss the chief differences between college and their previous schooling. The people who come to college want to work, to work successfully, and to reap the rewards—in marks, in self-satisfaction, in repayment for the help and encouragement of parents and teachers, in approval of the fraternity or sorority, in foundation for future work and future living.

What is orientation?

If the college whole-heartedly accepts the advantages of this initial motivation and accepts also the necessity for retaining this high level of aspiration, it accepts a responsibility not to disappoint and not to discourage. No college is going to reduce standards so that apparent success is possible for all. No college is obliged to remove all competition or to protect the weak to the point where goals for the strong become a mockery. The college's obligation is something more difficult: to capture and hold the student's imagination, it must present its case with skill and scrupulous fairness to itself.

If the colleges listen to what the freshmen say, they cannot fail to see what an important part surprise has played in the disappointments encountered. Surprise at the expense of going to college, surprise at lacks and deficiencies in high school preparation, surprise at the need for new reading, writing, and study skills, surprise at high standards, surprise at requirements after college entrance. No freshman dean or counselor or instructor can afford to dismiss this surprise lightly. Undoubtedly it is a pity that first-year students are unrealistic. But the college *cannot* afford to let their dawning recognition of reality become disillusionment, or let the truth about college blind them to the fact that college may not be what they expected—it may be even better.

If the freshman curriculum has a rational purpose, the purpose should be presented to the student along with the list of required courses. If a liberal arts course has a reason for being—different from that of professional or vocational preparation—that reason or goal should be used to guide the freshman. If a college faculty is rethinking its procedures—if it is studying or experimenting in general education courses or integrated subjects—the students have a right to feel that they are partners in the investigation. The college has little to lose in revealing that it is an institution made up of human beings who are fallible, but who are earnest and devoted to the task of offering good education.

The important thing to realize is that academic adjustment is a personal matter. The professor who is used to shunting off to some guidance officer anything that looks like a personal or emotional problem may be forgetting that motives for work are problems—when they are unsatisfactory—but are the cause of the brilliant performance he loves to see—when they are effective. Motivation to stay in college, to work, and succeed, and enjoy college, is at the heart of academic adjustment. The double task of the college is to take advantage of the stimulation with which the student arrives, and to assure that it will live on in him as he gains a deeper understanding of what the college itself can mean.

THREE

On Their Own at Last

I

WHAT the freshman lacks is precedent. He has well established habits of reacting to those people who have in the past surrounded him, but he realizes that these are not precisely the patterns to apply in college living.

"I think it is impossible to adjust to college life instantly," says a freshman from one of the men's colleges. "Everyone encounters a certain homesickness and discouragement which, coupled with the problems of tackling college work and the natural uneasiness of starting a new adventure, often overburdens the student." Other students echo the refrain that "it takes time," or "You have to look around and decide what you want to do, which people will be your friends."

It would be foolish to try to maintain any artificial dichotomy between the young man's or woman's academic and personal lives. But it is evident that in some activities in college the academic or intellectual motives for attendance are uppermost, while in other situations the student is operating largely under the influence of his expectations in the personal or social area. What are some of his goals with regard to the group around him? To find friends, to deal effectively with the ordinary business of daily

44

living, to meet competition and challenge, to depend on himself for direction and decision, to follow up interests and avocations— at least these and probably many more. Each individual has his own concept of his goals, and his own standards of success; he also differs from other freshmen in the extent to which he is conscious of his objectives and his progress toward them. But even the least articulate boy or girl has his purposes in going to college and experiences fulfillment or frustration in some degree.

Rooming together

"Roommates are both a curse and a blessing," said one boy. The roommate keeps the newcomer from feeling complete isolation. Even incompatible souls are sharing some of the same experiences, and some recognition that all one's troubles are not unique usually results. On the other hand, many difficulties arise because of the loss of privacy, the need to consider others in various activities from sleeping to study schedules, and the obvious fact that sometimes the people sharing quarters are unsuited to one another.

One in a group of three can be the "odd man." One student is sure that the background of those sharing should be a matter of concern to the college. "I had roommate trouble. I was in with two boys from the same prep school, who used to have bull sessions until 2:30 A.M. on old times and old friends. No consideration. I'm convinced a freshman should never be bunked with two old buddies. It's a lousy feeling, not having anything in common with your roommates."

A girl reports on a combination of circumstances—and a combination of roommates—that might alarm anyone. Every indication is that her experience is unusual, for which others may be thankful. "Socially, my first experiences with college were mostly unpleasant. (I later found out that everyone was not like my first sample.) My roommates were quite a group the first semester.

One was a genius, I think, but partly neurotic (always crying). Another was failing, a third was foreign and understood very little English, and the fourth had insomnia and loved to have someone stay up and chat with her. There was no adequate place for us to study, since none could be done with five in the room. Unfortunately, too, the role of peacemaker fell to me. We do have housemothers, but they are such intellectual women that discussing such a problem with them seemed out of place. I finally did so, and the arrangements are much better this part of the year."

Some colleges assign roommates with care—going so far as to place students together who seem to be similar in interests and ability. Where possible, some assign single or double rooms according to the preference of the applicants. One college reports that it always informs the freshman of his future roommate's name and address, and encourages the two to get in touch with each other before college opens. An aim at this college is to mix students from differents parts of the country. Planning the assignment of rooms obviously puts a premium on adequate information about the personal characteristics, interests, and background of entering students.

It is worth while for the college to listen to what the freshmen say about this aspect of their community life. "Your roommate can be the big factor in getting along," said one northern girl in a college in the South. "Mine has had to hear about all my problems in learning about a new section of the country as well as a new college. Without her, I know I'd have headed for home after the first two weeks." A report on the negative side comes from a girl in a situation apparently forced on the college. "We were so crowded they had to put four of us freshmen in an upperclass dorm. It has been pretty horrible because we don't care any too much for each other, and we are simply *nothing* in the hall. Everybody else had her friends, and that, added to the fact that we had to keep freshman hours, meant it took weeks to feel as if we belonged anywhere."

Major differences in standards of conduct are intensified in the closeness of a room. One boy says, "There is no way to study in our room. My roommate is addicted to loud records and loud parties, except when he decides to catch up and works till 2 A.M. Both stages seem to be equally hard on me. I get along by studying in the library, but I went out for track and have to have my sleep." Drinking is mentioned by several students in men's colleges. "Maybe I'm just a 'creep,' but I don't drink and I object violently because my roommate insists on keeping liquor in the room, in spite of the rules." Another freshman says, "I learned to drink, in strict moderation, at home. It's the fellows who don't know how to do it, think it makes a 'big man' out of them, and habitually get potted that I can't take. I include my roommate. I'm disgusted and will be glad when I can move to the fraternity house."

Knowing how to start

Even though examples of minor tragedies and real difficulties could be multiplied, many freshmen pay tribute to the effectiveness of shared living for helping introduce the individual to this confusing group of his peers. It is easier to admit to uncertainties about social contacts, in formal or informal situations, when the doubts are exposed only to those who know you well. "Getting off on the right foot" is an anxiety for many freshmen. When to these normal hesitancies are added significant individual problems—membership in a minority racial or religious group, difference in cultural or economic background from most of the class, or major misconceptions about what to expect of a particular college—social relationships become critical. Yet the freshman is keenly aware of himself as an individual, even as he begins to sort out other individuals in the group.

On your own at last

The fact is that the freshman is surrounded by new demands, new people, and a structure of society different from any he has known. The new situation requires decisions he may never have needed to make before. Perhaps for the first time, he is initiated into managing his own finances, budgeting his time, pursuing his own interests, selecting his own friends. One student writes, "The real problem is that you have to know where you stand yourself. There is no other way to maintain your independence."

This lack of, or confusion in, personal objectives in life causes frequent comment. Over 40 per cent of the students in men's colleges, and about 30 per cent of those in colleges for women and in coeducational colleges say that they are troubled by such matters. One says, "I find myself worrying about things that never entered my head before—the purpose of my life, the fate of man, the validity of religion, and so on." "The main quality of which I am aware is my realization of responsibility and self-dependence." But many agree, too, with the girl who says, "Independence is certainly what I wanted, but now I realize I am unprepared for it." The college itself may appear as one of the actors in the scene. "I feel that the college stresses 're-evaluation of our basic values' too much—it certainly must be done but I believe it will come with time."

Further understanding of themselves comes to the freshmen as they criticize their classmates. Many students believe that they make their judgments from a firm basis in their own beliefs and standards. This may comfort observers who are alarmed lest the rethinking of values should cut too deeply into the standards of college youth. When the freshmen write of disillusionment with college, they trace it to the feeling that some classmates place educational and intellectual objectives too low, and that some have standards of social conduct with which they cannot agree.

Some express concern about the decline in church attendance among classmates or about lack of support for the college's religious program. Many of those who have become aware of their self-criticism emphasize that their own standards are still high and that now they hold to their conclusions through strong conviction, not just through habit.

College and home

Self-examination frequently leads to the conclusion that home and family are the source of inner security and the background of strength. Those freshmen who wrote about home or home community factors which, they believed, affected their adjustment to college, almost all praised early training—in independence, in sound values, in tolerance.

Recognition of this debt is frequently accompanied by a realization of the distance separating home from college. The total of those actually reporting homesickness is not large—only about 8 per cent—(although in women's colleges 15 per cent were aware of it as a difficulty). Worry about conditions at home is more frequently mentioned, being indicated by more than 11 per cent of the total group. A psychologist might point out that college students who had some hesitation in admitting that they were homesick might feel freer to admit to anxieties about the situation back home. Sickness at home strikes a special fear to the heart of the student who is far away and depends on mail and telephone for news. What threatens happiness and security "back there" is frightening and perplexing.

Another home worry is the financial one. This is checked by about 17 per cent of all freshmen. Financial concern bears especially heavily on students in colleges for men and those in co-educational institutions. Only about 10 per cent of the women identify this as a source of problems. But students of both sexes often state that their difficulties in keeping within a self-imposed budget are important because they recognize the sacrifices made by their families to provide money. Scholarship students are, not unnaturally, aware of finances and the ramifications of this problem for themselves and their parents.

Undoubtedly one reason for the emphasis the freshmen place on changing and rethinking social values is the feeling that the individual is doing his own deciding now. The process of studying one's own beliefs may be an anxious one, and is seen as such even by those who state that in the end they have returned to their original ideals with added conviction. Sometimes those who believe, rightly or wrongly, that they have now adopted more tolerant attitudes than those of their parents are uncertain that they will retain the approval of their families. One boy who says he went from a conservative town to a cosmopolitan college states, "I know I have made friends my parents wouldn't approve of." A commuting student says, "I know my family can't understand what is happening to me, and there is constant conflict between us on how I should spend my time, and so on." The first vacation can also bring a shock, as one boy found: "I had great difficulty in getting 'back in the slot' over the holidays. A bit bewildering as I don't seem to know my parents and friends as I used to."

II

But we are all different

The freshman feels the need to "find himself" at the same time that he finds his place among his classmates. Both parts of the process are at once personal and social matters. One learns to know people by living with them and watching them in the close familiarity of campus. One also learns to recognize the differences among them, to select among them, and to find those with whom one wishes to live and work most closely.

"Variety" seems to be the key word to describe the student body. And this variation, living with it and adjusting to it, provides the chief problem for many newcomers. Almost a third of the freshmen spontaneously mention the fact that just learning that there are so many kinds of persons in college was a considerable surprise. There are many positive statements about the value of learning to accept differences in economic and social background, in religion, in race or nationality. In some colleges, particularly those with religious affiliations, differences in faith are minimized, but comments on differences in personality, standards of thinking and conduct, and other factors are just as frequent as they are in colleges with more heterogeneous enrollments.

More about standards

It may be that freshmen are only beginning to learn tolerance. Whatever the reason, they are sometimes hard on each other, and on occasion downright disapproving. What seems to bother them most is excessive behavior of any sort—even too much studying. Drinking, irresponsibility regarding property, interference with the work or study of others, overemphasis on athletics or party life, all these are criticisms aimed by students at college groups. But they do not come in the form of blanket condemnation.

The college is a community

The college itself appears as a factor helping to determine the sort of world in which the freshman lives. At a minimum, the freshman is aware of the college as it sets up the regulations and enforcement of college discipline. Some young men and women apparently expect to find no external standards for conduct, but in fact freshman regulations range from the minimal to the rigid. At one college, a number of freshmen complain that restrictions covering dress, hours for social activities and study, and for class attendance are too formal and are administered in ways that do not promote maturity. At another, certain students feel that the college overestimates the desire of the newcomer for noninterference; some of these express a feeling of considerable insecurity.

The honor system, completely under student government control, which is in operation at one school was the occasion of many positive comments, but on other campuses there are as many objections that the student disciplinary committee is under faculty domination.

Colleges may wonder why the freshmen give more emphasis to individual and group standards and pressures than to the role of the institution itself. Is it the judgment of the college that it ought to be mostly a "silent partner" in setting the standards of the community? Or does the faculty believe that it should take an active share? What emerges from the freshman comments reveals that both the *laissez-faire* attitude and the provision of strong leadership are in fact expressions of policy, and that the influence of the adults is inescapable. Students speak of the "coldness" of one college or the "warm, interested atmosphere" of another. Neither is accidental.

Does the college reach the student?

Many problems of personal and social growth arise because students look on college as a way of life, and expect to derive from it most of the major satisfactions of the years they attend. Consequently, any circumstances which seem to divide them from the rest of the group, or that portion of it they select as their special province, emerge as sources of frustration. Too heavy a load of work for the student earning all or part of his expenses cuts into study time and may deprive the boy or girl of social benefits. Participation in a major sport—or a music curriculum making unusual demands for practice time—may result in a feeling that one's social contacts are too limited, and that increased social activity would consume time needed for study or sleep.

Physical separation from the college is, of course, an objective fact which cannot easily be compensated for. Commuters often feel that their college experience is less rich and complete than that of the resident student. Several colleges without boarding facilities sometimes appear to be more successful in drawing most members of their student body into a social and extracurricular program than are colleges where some commute and others do not. But one boy attending what he calls a "street-car" college had a reaction which indicates that the influence of the college can be minimal: "I don't know why you talk about freshmen as if they were unique. I'm just going on in school, under the same public school system, and for all I can see school is still just class periods and homework. I still live on the same block and have the same friends and activities as ever."

Commuting students all too often say, "Of course, I don't live at the college, so I may not have an adequate idea of what is done to make the boarding students feel a part of things." In addition to feeling out of things the commuting student may find that other elements in his personal life create difficulties. "The whole thing," says one, "is the problem of trying to compromise between home and college." Many commuters complain that their families find it hard to adjust to longer working schedules, the need to meet library and class hours, and the time desired for college events.

One university with coordinate colleges for men and women is a conspicuous example of what a conscious attack on the commuter's special case can do. One after another of its freshmen stress the full program for the inclusion of local students in activities, and they are loud in their praise of the housing arrangements which permit the nonresidents to stay overnight a dozen or more times a year.

III

Participation is the keynote

The testimony of the freshmen is that any force which divides the college group into uncommunicating fragments will create serious individual problems, and almost any activity which motivates sharing time and energy will aid in adjustment. The basic reason for the approval that students give to such diverse factors as "college spirit," club activities, church and chapel participation, community service, physical recreation programs, dances and parties, even mild forms of hazing and "ratting," is the development of true "belongingness," and the increase in meaningful contact with their peers.

What about fraternities?

Many men and women report that their fraternity or sorority has given them the greatest satisfactions of the year. They stress security within the group, motivation for scholastic as well as social progress, good living arrangements, and many other values. Why, then, does the fraternity system create problems, and does it create them for members as well as nonjoiners?

The consensus seems to be that wherever the clubs follow practices that shut some students out of the social, political, or recreational life of the campus, they will be criticized by the outsiders. The criticism is more acrid if the group of independents is small. A campus on which only half of the students join has a nonfraternity group large enough to exert pressures of its own and to keep some of the divisive elements in check.

The most frequent criticisms of fraternities are that they monopolize the social life of the school and that independents are excluded. There is some justification for these comments according to one dean. He admits that "we may not be paying enough attention to the social life of the boys. We turn it over to the fraternities and pay little more attention." Even though almost all students on this campus belong to societies, some freshmen comment that they lost friends made before pledging when they joined "fraternities which do not fraternize." Such policies may handicap the members as well as the nonmembers. On coeducational campuses, traditions of social activities lining up certain fraternities and sororities, excluding others, may have the same effect.

Campus politics often furnish a battleground for competing societies and for conflicts between the "Greeks" and the "barbarians." Political rivalry has far-reaching effects on campuses where the student organizations make decisions in fields ranging from the conduct of social events to student discipline. Certain colleges have also seen powerful fraternities act to sway student opinion on national questions such as race relations and the admission of students from minority groups. One freshman casts a sidelight on fraternity procedures: "Fraternity rating on this campus depends more on electing class officers and such than on wealth or athletics. I realize one reason I was 'rushed' by several societies is because I had already started on the student newspaper."

Sometimes new members are aware of pressure to participate in activities just for the sake of their societies. "We don't have many athletes, and I know my fraternity brothers wonder why I don't go out for track the way I did in prep school. So far, I've managed to avoid the issue because I just don't have the time." Sometimes the duties of the initiate fall in unexpected places. A scholarship boy reports, "I know it sounds like a joke, but I must say my fraternity has made a regular nuisance about my job in the college dining room. The brothers expect me to be sure they get the best of everything, and first service. Sometimes this really gets in my hair!"

Enthusiastic loyalty is often at its height in the second term of the freshman year. One girl points out that sorority membership solves some of the most pressing problems of the new student: "Many of my difficulties in finding friends and knowing what to do seem far in the past. As soon as I was pledged I had a whole group of sisters to turn to with any problem. There is always someone available to work or study with, and even to get me a date! Now I really feel I am taken care of." Freshman members praise the fellowship they have found, their closer identification with their classmates, their ability to depend on the membership for guidance in social and academic procedures. Only a small minority chafes under the restraint that may be laid on it in choice of friends or activity.

But there *are* fraternity problems, and it is important to note that they are spelled out by joiners as well as nonmembers. The selection of some members inevitably implies the exclusion of others. "Something has gone out of the freshman class—I can only call it 'campus spirit'—now that we are split up into pledge groups." One society has been weighed against another: "I joined the only fraternity I could possibly agree with here. I was genuinely shocked at the discrimination against Jews and other groups which was clearly displayed by all the others." The emotional pitch of the rushing period mounts because of fears of not making the right choice, fears of not being asked at all. "Certainly you get a different picture of the sorority during rushing, when everyone is being as nice as possible to you. A mature girl ought to realize everything can't be quite *that* perfect." "The students and faculty split on the question of delayed rushing. Personally, I doubt if you can ever be sure of your selection until things are back to normal. Then it's too late. I am in favor of either delayed rushing or 100 per cent rushing, but this attitude is unpopular in my fraternity."

Selection and rejection. The snobbishness of wealth, or family background, or athletics, or personal popularity. The pernicious and soul-destroying policy of excluding classmates because of race or religion. Division of a campus into "accepted" and "non-accepted" groups. These are charges brought against the fraternities and sororities—not by outsiders, but by the freshmen themselves. Let the students speak: "In many ways I respect this college, and shall hate to leave it. But the bias and discrimination shown in the fraternity system is such that I cannot stay. I know that the slightest move I make will be an excuse for me to be blacklisted within the society, and I am going to transfer." "Any chance of my adjusting here has been so much affected by my being Jewish that I realize I am better off in the dormitory where I can concentrate on studies and not try to buck the pressure of a fraternity." "Belonging to a fraternity here is just an excuse for moving with the 'fast crowd.' The fraternities are powerful enough to get away with murder when it comes to liquor and wild parties—and I do mean wild." "Fraternity parties here are just brawls, and if you don't belong, as I don't, you have no social life whatever." One thoughtful girl sums it up in this way, "I can't get over the way some girls have been absolutely broken up by not making a sorority. They have lost confidence in themselves and in the college, and some of them just never seem to recover."

The freshmen give no final answers about the ultimate fate of the fraternity system. They show unequivocally, however, that this is a problem for the college as well as the individual societies. The fiction that fraternities are not really part of the college can no longer be maintained. The pretense that fraternities exist *at* a college but are not *of* it has been demolished by tragedies at initiations, by educational casualties when students leave college to escape fraternity pressure, and by the innumerable difficulties created for the adjustment of even those freshmen who are not critically damaged.

The college does not select its students for educational promise only to have them exposed to other selection standards which run directly counter to the aims of the institution. These social and personal matters are of direct concern to education, and colleges cannot escape the consequences of recognizing this fact. The boy or girl who is lost to his college because of discrimination or rejection in the social structure of the college is just as truly a victim of the "college system" as the student who fails because of inept teaching or a lockstep curriculum.

Hazing

Colleges, according to the freshmen, tolerate other practices which shut off individuals or whole classes from the rest of the student community. The "hazing" of the incoming class—especially when this takes the form of long-standing domination by upperclassmen—provokes considerable resistance. Hazing which involves physical rather than psychological pressures has been restricted to a minority of colleges in the last few decades. But the remnants of class hostility still create problems. As one student says, "The freshman who is uncertain or lonely to begin with feels just that much more isolated when older students appear only as taskmasters."

The several situations in which hazing is carried to extremes illustrate the dangers. One boy says, "Actually, 'hazing' is not limited to freshmen, but includes the domination of the whole social and personal life of the college man by the oldest students. When a class gets to the sophomore year, it merely has a chance to seek revenge on the incoming group." Performing unnecessary or annoying tasks for older students, preserving an artificial and rigid system of privileges and rights, can make the whole college an antidemocratic institution, at least outside the classroom. One student says, "I realize hazing isn't supposed to interfere with the academic part of life here. Actually, when you get so mad every time you step out of a lecture hall or go to eat a meal, you don't have enough energy left to concentrate on studying."

A major criticism made by students at one college is that an unhealthy dishonesty is practiced for the benefit of outsiders. "All this hazing is done with the avowed purpose of training in leadership and fellowship. But it goes much beyond this to an opportunity for downright cruelty and treachery. Complaining to a professor or anyone off campus would be an invitation to disaster." The results, as one student sees them, are inevitable. "I am among the students who are planning to leave college at the end of the year. I won't be a second-class citizen on any campus." Another points out, "A very good percentage, about half the freshman class, usually leaves after one semester. This situation should be changed for the good of the school."

What makes a problem serious? Hazing as vigorous as that described by the freshmen quoted above exists on few campuses, and involves a relatively small percentage of students. But the lessons to be learned from hazing apply to all students. The individual should not be exposed to either neglect or persecution in order to secure a higher education. His problems in learning to live with others—in learning to build a *community* out of the individuals attending a college, so that he and others are bound together by purpose, not just by physical proximity—should be part of his education. The person who is in serious need of help is not necessarily the one who has a large number of problems, but often the one whose problems are unknown or overlooked. Even if debilitating homesickness, or hazing, or social rejection affects only a few students, the college cannot ignore the opportunity to remove an obstacle to their success. But whether the difficulty is widespread or not, if the student knows that progress can be made, and is not left to feel that he is alone in a hopeless situation, then even the obstacles to adjustment can be occasions for learning and for establishing a sounder basis for the future.

IV

Boy meets girl

Building a full life at college should include making friends with persons of the opposite sex. At the coeducational and co-ordinate colleges such contacts grow naturally and informally. But in separate colleges, particularly in colleges for women, the institution itself is apt to take a more active part in helping solve the problems of social contact. Of the freshmen who commented on this point, about half felt that in their colleges a normal social life was possible if the student made some effort at finding it. About 30 per cent, however, felt that their colleges were too isolated, either geographically or through a policy of exclusiveness. One out of five believed there was too much emphasis on dating and mixed parties, with a few complaining that many of their classmates went overboard in an effort to attract attention from members of the other sex.

Standards and habits vary. "I discovered I had drifted into a group with much more expensive habits than I could meet. Some of the fellows feel a car is an absolute necessity, for example. And I certainly wouldn't let myself take such an extreme attitude." This boy goes on to state that he found plenty of classmates like him in finances, and he lost his self-consciousness as soon as he learned he could "still keep friends in both crowds." Many other freshmen emphasize the fact that "you have to feel your way," and that initial insecurity is normal. Comments that "I put too much emphasis on the social side," and that "It took time for me to learn college standards of dress and talk" point to the recognition that the college community has its own demands. Serious difficulties in budgeting time and attention to academic and social life are reflected in statements like this boy's: "I was a 'party boy' and even got to be a heavy drinker the first term. Now I'm on academic probation I realize I've gone to the opposite extreme and cut out all social life, but I guess I had to learn the hard way. Hope I'll get a chance to straighten it out next year."

Previous school experience, the customs of home and home community, and, of course, general maturity all play their part. A few boys and girls who went to high schools or preparatory schools in which the sexes were separated mentioned their need to acquire poise in working and playing in mixed groups. On the other hand, some of those in men's and women's colleges missed the give-and-take they found in coeducational high schools. A few men are "pleased not to have to bother with girls" during the serious business of going to class! The dean at a women's college says that she had a parallel comment from some girls. But separation should not involve complete isolation.

What is maturity?

An attempt to define social and personal maturity when it comes to dating, parties, and so on, is clearly one of the duties the student believes he must undertake. It may be all too easy to dismiss as "immature" any conduct which is not familiar or according to the standards of one's former friends. The term is applied by freshmen both to behavior which is more rigid and that which seems more relaxed than the student will accept for himself.

The comments on drinking and regulations concerning liquor on and off campus almost invariably stress the need for the individual to make his own decisions. "I admit I have been profoundly shocked at the drinking at the fraternities, particularly when women were invited for parties and dances. But I feel the best solution is just for me to stay away." Another boy concludes, "Most freshmen who drink seem to think they have to in order to be popular." One girl believes she has found the solution: "I don't like to drink, and I have discovered that if I can suggest somewhere to go that has records and dancing without liquor my dates are glad to find a new spot, too."

The questions raised by the freshmen are not always answered. "I think the fraternities and the college ought to take a stand on drinking. The students talk about it, but if it never comes up for real decisions, there isn't much accomplished." There is strong support for permitting students to make their own choices, and stress on the maturity needed so that they can regulate their own conduct. There is a feeling that group standards and pressure for conformity should not be allowed to override individual conscience. But, as implied by the boy who believed the college should "take a stand," students also believe in thorough discussion of social problems, *with the adults at the college taking their share.*

Drinking is stressed as a particular aspect of the problem of social conduct. "One's point of view on the use and abuse of liquor is always a topic of conversation in the dorm." But the total matter of social adjustment is more complex. Far more serious, from the point of view of the majority of students, are actions which reject or isolate people, some traced to the fraternity system, but many based on general intolerance of major differences in race, family background, or personality. The students who are concerned to see these practices applied to others rightly consider them moral problems. Those who feel the discrimination are bitter or bewildered.

Many students seem to feel that personal and social problems can be solved only by the student himself, and are reluctant to believe the college may have a role to play. One says, "I am not sure about the term 'college's provisions for freshmen.' I think they have been sufficient, even to the point of sympathetic understanding of problems. My being of Oriental descent has a bearing on my nonacademic life. I lived in the Territory all my life, and mixed with other races freely. There isn't any outright discrimination here, but I admit that the continual feeling of some 'differentness' is wearing. I don't believe in that 'isolation' attitude at all, but I realized how much it had affected me later. When I did get into social affairs on vacation, I was suddenly lacking completely in self-confidence. I repeat my opinion and strong feeling, however, that it is up to the individual in almost every situation to at least try to handle and understand matters in an adult manner. I wanted to come to college and I want to finish. I have hope for a better future."

FOUR

Who Is This Freshman?

I

Discussing the various phases of academic, personal, and social adjustment results in a sort of compartmentalization which, however useful, is unrealistic. For the central figure in this study is the whole student, in all his complexity, personal and social. What kind of a figure, then, emerges when the man or woman is taken "in the round"? Some clue may be found in the student analyses presented on the following pages.

There is an adage that says, "All the world's a little queer excepting me and thee, and sometimes I think thee's a little queer, also." The freshmen here quoted are definitely individual. Two of them are somewhat hostile to elements of the college situation in which they find themselves, one is enthusiastic to the point of being perhaps uncritical, while the fourth appears to have given an unusual amount of attention to the analysis of his surroundings. They do not pretend to be "representative" of anyone but themselves. They are introduced here primarily because their replies give a graphic idea of the young persons behind this book.

Is age the real problem here?

The first boy is one of a small group of students permitted to enter college before completing four years of high school work.

Like others in this situation, he was selected as a person of unusual academic promise. Most of his difficulties, he relates, are in the area of social adjustment, and he pinpoints the relation of age to fraternity membership as typifying his problem. A discerning reader, however, will wonder if his lack of adjustment is not considerably more complex than this, in origin and in result.

I feel high school work was designed for average and subnormal students. I loafed through high school and found that college requires a higher standard of work a little bit too late. My high school English preparation was very poor, but I made the advanced English class because I have done a lot of reading on my own. For anthropology at college I have one of the world's leading anthropologists—but he can't teach. However, I can honestly say I like the work here.

My major disillusionment concerns my picture of college boys. I thought that at last I would find an intellectual atmosphere and some well-bred companions. At [this college] I have found little of either. For most of my fellow-students, college is a joke—a free loaf on papa's dough! College to them means social activities, the courses are only there to annoy them. Drunkenness is admired and on weekends is common. Was also disturbed by freedom of action concerning other people's belongings.

I had an upbringing where the emphasis was placed on academic rather than athletic achievement. Moreover, speaking your mind was not frowned upon. Telling people what I thought of them and of other things has made me unpopular.

My second disillusionment concerns fraternity members. I was astounded at the type of people that most fraternities wanted. I wouldn't think of associating with them, and there are five out of the eleven houses I wouldn't join even if they bid me. My disillusionment with the men who were taken in made me very much disappointed when I wasn't bid by a fraternity even though they took in those my mental and social inferiors. I later found out it was because of my age, none of them wanted to take a chance on a "15-year old kid." Happily I have been assured of getting several bids next year, and I don't think that not making a fraternity my freshman year is going to handicap me. Fraternities up here are in the position of being vital to advancement. Unless you are in one you don't stand a chance of acceptance.

I thought they came to learn

The second student, as he says, came from a metropolitan area. His college has evidently afforded him some surprises, particularly about the values placed on different aspects of college life. He tends to generalize, rather than giving the details of what he finds, but it seems clear that while he prizes individual thinking generally, this tolerance does not necessarily extend to opinions and pressures with which he does not agree.

Some (but not all) of my college work is on a more mature level than that at my high school. The quality of teaching as a rule is much better. As for interest and satisfactions, there is a tremendous difference. I came to college to learn, and most of the courses are good. Some of them have been outstanding because the professors are educators of the first water, and very warm persons, besides.

College brought the big disillusionment: I thought men came to college to learn, to have an intellectual experience, to become scholars. They don't. They come to get a degree, go to parties, get high marks while doing as little work as possible, etc. I found strong anti-intellectual currents; there is strong pressure for conformity—very strong pressure. At times one has to make the choice between losing his personality completely in the mass, or relying upon whatever intestinal fortitude he might have to stick by ideals he believes in. I'm still not sure what kind of a man I am.

It took me quite a while to make friends; I'm not a very outgoing person. I have found boys whom I like, though, and I'm glad I'm joining a fraternity even though I think on a campus as small as ours they divide up a class too much. They set up even harsher standards of conformity and increase social differentiation.

I don't think my school or anyone else could have prepared me for this. I had to find out for myself that everyone wasn't a New Yorker, and that there were lots of different kinds of people in the world.

What are the signs of good adjustment?

How is good adjustment characterized? Does it mean uncritical acceptance of all phases of college life? Does it require ideal circumstances? Or can it appear in an attitude of tolerance, recognition of shortcomings, and a constructive attitude toward the improvement of one's *alma mater?*

There are no final answers. Effective adjustment can undoubtedly take as many individual forms as maladjustment. Occasionally, however, one finds a student whose choice of college seems to have worked out unusually well, and who is therefore an unhesitating advocate for almost every aspect of campus activity. The girl whose comments are summarized next even has a good word to say about two unpopular subjects—commuting and hazing. She may have accepted everything a little too readily, as she herself remarks, but she may well be a pleasure to have around—in class and out—because of her outgoing habits of participation.

I was fortunate enough to attend a big high school, but one that has a good record of college preparation. I have not had too much difficulty with college work, except that there is so much of it, and I am a procrastinator, so I have had to work hard to get it all in.

The new experimental curriculum is, in my opinion, excellent. It makes many standard lecture courses for freshmen seem pallid by comparison. Essentially, it consists of applying the seminar technique to the various "general distribution" courses. There is no general pattern of teaching, however, because all the professors seem to have such strong ideas on how to approach their topics that they are all different. I am well satisfied with mine. In fact, college seemed like a whole new intellectual world for me.

Making friends has seemed easier than in high school, because my college is actually smaller, and at least mentally, we are more homogeneous. The one thing that is not wonderful is that I am living at home. Dormitory life *per se* has no great attraction for me, since I have more freedom and privacy at home. Yet there are so many people I should like to know better, and the only way to really know a person is to live with her.

On the other hand, since I am a communter, I belong to a large and active commuters' organization, and have a few friends and many acquaintances who are upperclassmen. The residents are in separate houses for freshmen and with the exception of junior counsellors assigned to each freshman, most of them don't know any upperclassmen.

I am extremely glad I chose a coordinate college. I have the environment and extracurricular activities of a girls' school and at the same time the social life found at coeducational colleges.

Hazing is limited to a brief period at the beginning of the year. I enjoyed it immensely. As far as I am concerned, it seemed to fulfill its objectives nicely. It brought the different freshmen into a group, and it even helped us find friends among the upperclassmen. I admit that although it was of the harmless variety (mismatched costumes, obsequious behavior, etc.), some of the freshmen disliked it intensely. They were attempting to adjust to a strange, new life, and they went through agonies of embarrassment when performing their pride-pricking stunts. I had an advantage in living at home. As a result, I had fewer worries, more poise during the first weeks, and could enter these activities with relative enjoyment. I think that for most freshmen it was a success.

I have found, to my disgust, that I usually become more enthusiastic about things than other people do, but I have found my freshman year a great satisfaction, and am delighted with life at college.

The fourth student is also an enthusiastic sponsor for his college, but feels that he and his classmates have legitimate criticisms of the way their life is organized. His interest in the academic as well as the social side of the college speaks for itself. He looks ahead to even more self-direction and responsibility.

Of course I came to college full of hopes and expectations concerning the work. Luckily, I had pictured college fairly accurately and thus had been prepared somewhat for the many adjustments. My work, I find, is not much more difficult than prep school work; it is the methods of study and the methods of presentation that differ—more note-taking, less class time, and much more of the figuring out left to the student. I have been assigned a very good percentage of excellent instructors, and all seem to be more than adequate, even when I'm not so sold on them personally.

The problem of budgeting time so as to fit in many of the phases of college life is perhaps the hardest pill for the freshman. Chances are that in high school he had time to fit in all the outside activities he wanted and still get good marks. In college a wider variety of activities is offered, they take more time, and studies take more time also. After the beginning, almost everyone has to retrench some. But, I admit, the accent is on academics here.

I feel that the choice of one's friends, whether one goes into a fraternity or not, is very important. They are those with whom you talk over all the problems which arise, and it is their advice and judgment which you respect the most. A lot of group adjustment, aside from organized clubs, and so on, takes place in the common dining hall and in chance get-togethers. Religion and social values have very little effect on adjustment once you get to college. Moral values, surprisingly enough, are probably the most important single element by which a freshman picks his closer friends and the groups to associate with. These groups are by no means restrictive on the members, but they usually tend to have parties together and may be as large as 80 or 100 freshmen who travel together. They are people who feel much the same way about how they enjoy themselves and what they want to get out of social life. You see, I mean moral values in the most general sense.

There is only very slight division between the daters and non-daters at this men's college, and this is evident only in week-end activities.

I think most of the freshmen like it here, though everybody has a few criticisms he would like to make. Freshmen object to rigid and uniform schedules set up for work and wish they had more choice in the required subjects. The lack of individual freedom given in the academic area should be remedied by allowing more informality and flexibility of work in dorms, more cuts, and more extracurricular activities, which are all now restricted.

Socially, a more constructive freshman-sophomore rivalry should be attempted. Although physical hazing is out, I feel that it was carried to extremes by making some of the insecure more insecure. But it did much even as it was to help establish class unity and make people forget differences in previous background.

I think the most important way to prepare a high school senior for college is to lead him to anticipate and expect a change. The unexpected is what is difficult to adjust to, but if a student has heard about lecture courses, research work, living problems, and so on, he comes to college with more idea how he will have to adjust and is considerably more ready to make the transition.

II

Evaluation and adjustment

Both the freshmen and their colleges come to look on personal and social adjustment as a process requiring time. It takes time to make decisions about friendship. It takes time to correct false impressions, to correct "the tendency to over-extend yourself in extracurricular matters at first." Above all, it takes time for the new student to assess the realities of college life, and to compare them with his expectations. Some students unquestionably emerge from this process in a state of dejection and disillusionment. Says one boy, "College did not live up to my expectations, but I guess things never do." A girl writes, "Too many of my classmates look on college as a way of passing the time till they get married." Another says more specifically, "I feel other students live in the past or future, and believe that college is a very temporary part of life. I disagree. If you know why you come to college and what you hope it will prepare you for, you will give it the respect and importance it deserves."

The unavoidable conclusion is that evaluation is the most important task of the first year. Self-evaluation goes hand in hand with the evaluation of other students and their conduct, and with the evaluation of the college itself.

What is the freshman's concept of adjustment?

When freshmen say they feel they are adjusting well in college, what do they mean? If the emphasis is on self-evaluation, they mean that going to college is meeting their own goals and objectives for this period. The student who realizes that his major personal goal is for a stimulating intellectual life, but who finds himself out of step with his classmates or fraternity brothers because of this aim, rightly feels maladjusted. The individual who has a powerful urge to feel secure and unchallenged in his religious or social beliefs will be intolerant of the college or classmate that seeks to disrupt his attitudes. The freshman who is undecided about his aims, educationally or vocationally, will be unhappy if he finds himself surrounded by students who are well-adjusted to a curriculum that demands more dedication of purpose than he can give it. The undecided are badly placed in technical or teachers colleges, for instance, unless they manage fairly soon to accept the goals set up for such training.

There is a variety of concepts of social adjustment, just as there is a variety of viewpoints on adjustment to one's own goals. Certain freshmen identify social adjustment with conformity. They suffer from self-doubt and feelings of rejection if they believe they differ from their classmates—if they have less money, or different preferences about entertainment, or a more cosmopolitan set of friends back home. They feel that they have failed unless they agree with their fellow students, or at least a sizable segment of the campus population. Less anxious students nevertheless do not wish to be entirely alone. "I do not feel at home here. There are too few independent souls, and those who do think for themselves are such exaggerated individualists that I don't find them very likeable." Another student says, "I am glad this is a large college. There is always a big enough group of congenial souls so that you can find company if you don't want to follow along with the fast crowd or the egg-heads."

Many freshmen realize that the presence of a large group of students representing all shades of opinion, belief, and conduct, can be a great strength for the college and a great resource for the person who is growing up. "I can never be too grateful for this chance to meet people of all sorts," says one girl; "I feel that having to know them and get along with them will make me an altogether bigger person than I could ever have been if I had stayed home and taken a job—never been jolted out of my comfortable rut." But this does not mean undiscriminating acceptance of all people or all activities. A boy in a men's college comments, "There should never be too much pressure to belong to everything. I have met a number of men here who just can't be bothered, yet who are friendly in a quiet sort of way. They are well worth knowing because they take time to think about what they are going after. They are not just swept along." Conformity can be a response to the urge to hide, to be inconspicuous; or it can be a genuine acceptance of group standards. But it need not be elevated to a virtue in such a way that the individual "with a mind of his own" feels that good adjustment has no other characteristics.

What is the college's concept of adjustment?

As the college administration goes about its business—sets regulations for freshman conduct, decides on the methods and policies for student discipline, provides for adult guidance to individuals or groups of students—it also is expressing opinions about adjustment. Some colleges place academic success first to the extent that any individual is regarded as "well-adjusted" if he makes normal progress in his courses. Some colleges operate only on the "emergency" policy, holding that students should manage their own affairs outside the classroom, and that the college should intervene only in cases of obvious antisocial conduct. Others believe that the students and the patrons of the college hold the institution responsible for a considerable amount of direct control over the social and personal lives of the freshmen. Still others value conformity just as highly as do some students.

Many colleges control some aspects of student life, but leave other decisions to be made elsewhere. A college which will not permit religious bias in its admission pattern may allow fraternities to practice discrimination. Another may take great pains to provide a well-rounded program of social activities with nearby colleges, but overlook a rigid set of student cliques and social hierarchies.

College faculties can and do influence all phases of the life of the student body. The responsibility for determining how social and personal growth takes place is not to be shrugged off. *Lack of attention* is in itself a policy. According to the freshmen, the nonacademic side of the college is so vital that lack of adjustment to it can mean withdrawal from the school. The college must accept the fact that its function is to aid student growth, not merely to administer a curriculum. Education involves the whole person.

There is still plenty of room for colleges to differ in their decisions about how to promote maturity. There will always be freshmen who require the security of a well-regulated environment and freshmen who must be treated with the utmost respect for their need to direct themselves. But the adults at the college must act honestly to examine what they are doing and why they are doing it. Then the differences between colleges can become instruments of guidance.

FIVE

Focus on Guidance

I

THE VERY act of going to college seems to precipitate difficulties. As one freshman boy said, "I guess I came to college to 'find myself.' Even so, I didn't realize how important it would seem to do it all at once—decide what kind of courses I wanted to take, make up my mind where I was going vocationally, and still find time to make friends and learn what kind of a person I am and what I think about moral and social questions!" This is a large order. But these questions must be resolved if the student is to work effectively in college and plan sensibly for his future.

The value which freshmen place on their new independence leads many of them to look to themselves and their own resources as the primary aid in solving initial problems. The college administration is, as a general rule, equally anxious to deal with self-directing individuals, and tends to encourage students to think or work their way out of their difficulties whenever possible. Is this realistic? How far can the freshman go with his own judgment and insights? What equipment does he need to help him?

The academic demands of student and college

Academic problems often make their appearance even before classes start. Taking placement tests, learning about freshman requirements, selecting first-semester courses, and going through the procedure of registering (itself a considerable hazard in some universities) consume a good deal of time and energy at the outset. Often those very activities designed to complete the induction of the student into college also cause him to ask his first questions. Why does the college require tests at this point? Haven't I already been admitted? Why do I have to take courses in math, languages, or contemporary civilization? Why do I have to take a course in chemistry when I just completed one in my senior year? Haven't I already been "prepared" for college?

The sectioning of classes may be another source of doubt about high school and college standards. The former valedictorian of a high school class reported that she was much distressed at being assigned to the "slower" section of an English course. And more searching questions, obviously, emerge after the first marks are received.

One of the college deans makes an appropriate comment: "The task of relating one's self realistically to college standards is a difficult one for some students. Some insist that their relative standing among college students should be exactly the same as that they enjoyed in the more heterogeneous group of high school companions and are disposed to lay the responsibility for their lower marks on the faculty. In some cases, family pressures and demands are even more unrealistic than the ideas of the students themselves."

It is a rare college entrant who can set his academic aims for the first year or more of college unguided, and do so with the assurance that his expectations will be achieved. Most graduates leave high school with scanty information about themselves and their abilities and shortcomings. Their definite knowledge is probably limited to their high school marks and the fact that they met the entrance standards of their college. If they are attending a college which admits any graduate of the accredited schools of a state, the second item of information adds nothing to the first.

Tests of ability given in high school, and results on entrance and placement tests for the college, are frequently regarded as so confidential that the student is not taken into the secret. Obviously, if such data are discussed with students, they must be presented with enough material for sound interpretation, and must be handled with great care. Lacking such a thorough approach by the guidance department, results alone will probably do more harm than good. The fact remains, however, that the student usually misses out on much of the help that might be given him through careful counseling about his own aptitude and achievement. From this uncertainty about his own equipment and the standards he will face in college stems much of his need for assistance in even beginning his academic adjustment.

What is the goal?

Many students believe their difficulties are aggravated by confusion about educational and vocational goals. One of the college deans points out that freshmen often do not realize that lack of definite vocational plans is common for persons of their age, and also do not correctly estimate the value of college in exploring further before they decide on a field of work. He says: "Some freshmen handle the problem of indecision in this matter quite well, generally accepting the fact that they need time, and the kind of self-knowledge that their college education should help them to get. . . . But there are others . . . who cannot accept the situation philosophically, and insist they have a right to be unhappy and relatively unproductive because they 'don't know where they are going,' comparing themselves wistfully with the pre-meds."

Personal evaluation

If the student is handicapped in planning to avoid academic maladjustment, he may be completely at a loss to judge what will happen to him in the social and personal realm. The effects of the rupture with his previous environment can range all the way from slight difficulty to serious emotional upheaval. He may need all the stability of his personality to keep his head, and he will appreciate any previous experience in facing new groups and learning to live away from the reassuring presence of people and places already known. If the old signposts—the assumptions one makes about how people will react and what one's own response will be—no longer give the student an accurate course to follow, he needs help in navigating.

The student helps himself

Yet the student can and does guide himself to a remarkable extent. The individual who is already off to a good start, whose precollege experience has been, by and large, enjoyable and successful, finds that many difficulties can be taken in stride. Habits of reacting positively and experience in facing new situations realistically are traits which have a good chance of persisting. The boy who concluded that the best preparation for college was "the kind of person you are and have been" made an accurate observation.

Everyone can think of individuals whose adjustment is outstanding in spite of an environment and experience which for most people would result in collapse or disintegration. But within the normal or average range of occurrences, the ones which help in college are those which helped before. In the area of academic work, one is more likely to find good achievement from those who learned well before than from those who have major uncorrected scholastic weaknesses. Some of the aspects of high school preparation are not under the control of the student, who can do little about the quality of teaching or counseling provided by his school. But the individual who has taken full advantage of his earlier opportunities is likely to be able to take initiative in finding solutions for problems when he is on his own. If his secondary school background has given him good training through courses, activities, and counseling, he is at an advantage.

A tribute to the home

More than half the freshmen questioned reported that their home and family background helped their adjustment to college. Perhaps the students who believed that their homes had hampered rather than helped did not feel free to discuss such an influence, even anonymously. At any rate, nearly all those mentioning home life stressed its positive contribution. Such freshmen were strengthened by the knowledge that they were loved and respected. The family had confidence in the ability of the individual to make his own decisions wisely. The home had attitudes favorable to the value of education. Repeatedly the freshmen said, "Being allowed to think and make decisions, and establish a certain mental independence without losing my family's confidence, helped much in accepting college for what it is." "My parents were so sensible. They left the decision of whether I wanted to go to college, and what college, in my hands. I do not mean to say they showed no interest. On the contrary, they helped me look over information about colleges and took me to visit them. But no one forced my hand."

Many of those who felt most secure were those who believed they had sound moral and ethical values. Home, home and church, school, older friends and relatives, and organizations like service guilds or youth groups, were usually mentioned as the source of these values. But one freshman warned against rigidity. "I certainly still hold to my own values. But I think it is a great mistake to judge another student whose standards are different because of different upbringing, religion, and so on. When people have had their feelings hurt in the arguments at the dorm on topics like this, it happened because some of the girls insist their way is the only right way without realizing that other people have been thinking about these problems, too. It's not the fact that someone differs from you that hurts, it's the implication that any right-thinking person *must* agree."

Practice in responsibility

Experienced teachers say that in order to make sure that what is taught in one situation will carry over into another, the student must become aware of the common elements in the two. Learning to reason in one course will help reasoning in another if the pupil is aware of why the same type of approach may work. The college freshmen, in the same way, stressed parallels between earlier life and college. Boarding school graduates said social adjustment was much easier since they had previously gone to live with a group of strangers. Camp experience played the same role for others. Moving from one town to another gave useful training. Even so, a few preparatory school graduates said that they had to adjust to the lack of supervised study time and the freedom from close restraints on absence from dormitories, and so on. While both school and college provided continuity in a "twenty-four hour" environment, the degree of responsibility encouraged for twelfth graders in some schools was markedly less than that needed the first year of college.

Many examples were given of activities which bore fruit in increased independence. If these freshmen were to give advice to prospective students, they would stress belonging to clubs in school, working with organizations for community service, joining similar groups in church, and participating in social functions as well. Some mentioned the need to work with adults as well as with other young people. Casual social contacts and mere school attendance were not sufficient to give experience in *purposeful* enterprises.

II

Self-guidance is part of education

The colleges as well as the young men and women depend on the maturity and the self-directing qualities which the student brings with him. Some colleges have a relatively limited program for aiding the freshman, and evidently believe that those who can survive the first year with a minimum of assistance are the best ones to retain for later years. In those colleges, failures and withdrawals are blamed on the students. Others believe that their selection procedures have resulted in a class which is all worthy of graduation, and that help should therefore be forthcoming wherever it is indicated. But colleges without exception expect students to use initiative in understanding themselves and their difficulties.

We have been trying to develop facilities for dealing with genuine problems of maladjustment when they occur, and, as far as possible, to remove potential causes for poor adjustments [says one dean]. On the other hand, both faculty and administration are keenly sensitive to the dangers of paternalism in this area, a paternalism which may rob the student of the legitimate personal demands which call for basic self-reliance. It is not easy to implement such a policy, particularly in the freshman year. The freshman is young, relatively limited in experience and judgment, and hence does need wise guidance at certain points. From a broader perspective, however, what we try to do, and hope to do more successfully as time passes, is to provide an atmosphere in which the student will find the stimulus to draw upon his own resources for the resolution of his problems, and thus for the maturing of his mind and character.

What counseling is available?

The word "counseling" is related to the idea of "consulting," and college counseling deals with the provision of methods for bringing the student together with individuals who will talk with him about his problems, or at least his procedures, in adjusting to his life at college. Exactly what the counselor does, how extensive or brief is his usual contact with the student, and how important he ultimately becomes as a factor in the student's development, varies from one college to another. The structure of the relationship depends on the administration's estimate of the guidance the college can and should furnish. Nothing goes farther to set the tone of the college environment than this decision about the place of guidance in education.

Variations in academic counseling

At its bare minimum, the task of the counselor or adviser is primarily an *academic* one. Part of the adviser's task is information-giving. He informs the student of the curricular choices open to him, tells him about the assignment of courses and class hours for his first term, and helps him select courses—if any electives are open to him. He plans ahead with the student for the selection of a major field of study, if such a selection has to be made early in the college career. If certain sequences of courses for a major field are required, he checks to see that the student follows the sequence.

This minimum outline of what the counselor does in the academic area looks most inadequate to some colleges. If the college does not have a required freshman program, the task of counseling is more complicated. For example, one college believes that "the program of studies that is individually designed by student and counselor calls forth greater interest and effort than the usual battery of required courses." Such a responsibility is obviously much heavier, for both adviser and student, than exists at the college with a program into which all freshmen are channeled.

If the freshman year is planned individually, the counselor needs more information about the student than he does if the freshman has relatively little deciding to do. At the college just mentioned, "The counselor already knows whatever the college knows about the student from her written records and summary of her admissions interview." If the student's choices are few at the start of the freshman year, the adviser may receive a less thorough introduction to the student, and rely more heavily on the information that becomes available through performance at the college. In such a case, college guidance may proceed with such a break from the school that the tremendous value of the information on academic and personal growth which has been collected in the preceding twelve years may be overlooked.

Other roles for the counselor

What has been said about variations in academic counseling applies with equal force to counseling in personal problems, and to counseling for vocational plans. Conclusions about the adequacy of the services must be made in terms of the goals the college has for its freshmen.

The college which prefers to set down strict social regulations for its students may reduce the personal advisory services mainly to a disciplinary function, taking the point of view that, once the student knows of the regulations, he can choose to abide by them, or choose to leave. Some colleges transfer much of the responsibility for inducing social conformity to upperclassmen. In a college where severe hazing is the custom, this amounts to a "pecking order," where the freshman has few rights to freedom of activity, the sophomore has a few more, and so on. Under such a situation, the upperclassmen are jealous of their privileges and see to it that the neophytes are kept strictly within bounds. In other colleges where the restrictions on the students are also rather noticeable, but where the aim is conformity and discipline for the sake of protecting the student from being distracted from his work, regulations may be enforced with sympathy and understanding.

Still other colleges hold more liberal attitudes about the degree to which they should control the conduct of freshmen. One large institution maintains little nonacademic contact with its students. It has confidence in the "sink or swim" theory, and expects the student to manage his own affairs, and to seek help from the college if he needs it. A small college believes the freshman should be left to "her own devices within the assumed confines of a sensible, acceptable way of going about her personal affairs and a general code of civilized conduct agreed upon by the college community." But this college counts on its advisory system to bind together its educational plan, holding to a goal that combines the academic and other areas into one; the goal is that "each student enter at once upon a course of study that has meaning for her and that she have immediately a continuing association with some experienced adult who is, within reason, always accessible and who can supply both understanding and competent advice. . . . [The student's] work is the core of the relationship; but to the degree that it becomes spontaneously possible, any or all other matters of moment enter into the conferences which are educational in the widest sense."

Who does the counseling?

The college's attitude toward guidance may be of more importance to the individual student than are such factors as the exact structure of the guidance services, or even the precise regulations laid down for freshmen. This emphasis on the spirit in which counseling is done should not, however, lead to the conclusion that if people are kind, helpful individuals, and are brought into close contact with the students, the college automatically has a good guidance program.

In many colleges, a great deal of effort goes into deciding who should carry the burden of counseling. Not all teachers are necessarily interested in establishing close personal contacts with a group of strange freshmen. Many faculty members, quite naturally, feel more competent to give academic advice than to aid in the personal and social development of new students. Others prove invaluable to a group of devoted students majoring in their field, but are impatient with the intricacies of helping to work out course programs for freshmen whose interests lie elsewhere or whose capabilities are only partly known. Few college teachers have had training as counselors, a fact which lends unusual importance to the training programs with which a few colleges are experimenting.

How does he know the student?

No skilled interviewer could expect to secure all the information necessary for advising a freshman soundly from one brief session at registration time. He needs first of all the help of the high school. Attention must be paid to all the earlier school has learned: "The fundamental purpose of qualitative assessments of the student's preparation, of his course records of academic progress, of estimates of ability, and of all the other data going to the college, is to provide a basis for the next steps in guidance. Without adequate secondary school records, the college selecting among candidates can never be sure that it has the information it needs to construct a picture of the whole candidate . . . [and] crucial decisions about his best placement within the college require the same kind of information needed for selective admissions."[1]

How well the counselor actually knows the student will also depend on how often the two meet and how many conflicting assignments the adviser may have. Frequency of contact between counselor and student ranges from once a term to once a week. The most usual pattern provides for at least one meeting of student and adviser each term, leaving extra talks open to the stu-

[1] Traxler and Townsend, *op. cit.*, p. 31.

dent's initiative. Frequently the freshman is required to see his counselor an extra time or two if his academic work is unsatisfactory, and some colleges expect the counselor to act on his own initiative if the student shows signs of difficulty in personal or social adjustment.

On other campuses, however, the counseling procedures are fragmented; whereas the adviser has general charge of academic planning, emergencies in either the scholastic or social areas may be handled by the deans. Such a college can be charged with thinking more about the structure of the counseling system than about growing, living freshmen. As one girl says, "I feel as if no one really knew me. My adviser is very sound in my major field, but she is such an intellectual woman I could never take any of my 'problems' to her."

If any college expects a continuing, important relationship between the student and his adviser, the adviser can take on such responsibilities for only a limited number of students. The "counseling load," in the colleges participating in the study, ranges in number of advisees per counselor from about five to forty. Even though the advisory services for those freshmen who are "only one in forty" are not necessarily inadequate, the advice is apt to be limited primarily to course selection and other academic matters, while the student is expected to use other resources for other types of consulting.

Specialized services for counselor and student

Many teachers are excellent counselors. Their personal qualities, interest in students, knowledge of freshman problems, and ability to guide rather than dominate the student make many of them outstanding. They are for the most part, however, realistic about their own training and knowledge, and do not think of themselves as experts in guidance. Even deans of students, with preparation and experience which is more specialized, are aware of the need of assistance in trying to solve certain problems of learning and adjustment.

Both academic and vocational guidance may require information about the student which has not been provided by the testing and analysis done in the high school or at college entrance. A detailed study of the freshman's abilities may be needed to help him select wisely among the major fields of concentration in college work. His vocational interests may be an important field for exploration to supplement data on his capacity. His reading skills may need further analysis if he is to improve his readiness to carry college work. Individual testing in the area of intelligence or personal characteristics may be indicated. To serve needs such as these, the college or university may include, or have access to, a variety of specialized organizations such as a testing bureau, a psychological clinic, or a reading clinic. The staffs of these groups may perform counseling functions themselves, or the information may be gathered and given to the regular adviser for interpretation to the freshmen. Even if some of the individual counseling is done by the specialist, the college counselor may still carry on the task of relating the work of the clinic to the other adjustments the student is making, or all the advisers may work as a team.

Trained individuals, as well as special service groups, are also a recognized adjunct to the counselors in some colleges. Medical services are usually part of the regular provisions of a college, but frequently there is not a sufficient coordination of medical and guidance services. Vocational counselors, psychologists, and psychiatrists or psychiatric counselors are more often in close contact with the personnel services of the institution, since their entrance into the work of most colleges has been secured through the interest of the group dealing with student adjustment.

In many instances, it becomes the duty of the counselor not

only to use the help of special clinics or individual consultants but also to make the student aware of the existence of these services and others which are of potential aid. Even at colleges in which special offices or clinics are organized, many students are not aware of the existence of any counseling services except academic advice. It is apparent that communications within these colleges have broken down.

III

Does the program reach the students?

The academic advisory system is both best known to students and most frequently used by them. About four out of five of the freshmen reporting thought the academic counseling was at least adequate; more than half thought it was good or excellent. About two-thirds thought the advisory services for personal or for vocational problems were at least adequate. Yet about 14 per cent of the freshmen reported that they were simply not aware that the college offered any counseling in personal problems, and over 16 per cent knew nothing about help in vocational guidance. About 15 per cent of the group thought counseling on personal adjustment was inadequate, and a similar percentage said vocational advisory services were insufficient. More than half of the freshmen said they had used the counseling services a great deal or at least to an extent which was about average. But more than a quarter had consulted with college advisers rarely or not at all.

Informal use of the college for guidance

Students who reported where they had turned for help gave a somewhat more favorable picture of the activity of the college staff than appears at first glance. The freshmen evidently interpreted the expression "counseling" to cover only the regular conferences with an individual adviser assigned to the student. Talks with deans, meetings with chaplains or other spiritual advisers, out-of-class contacts with teachers, and many other encounters, whether formal appointments or not, actually served counseling purposes. One boy spoke warmly of the guidance he had received from the coach of his team. Several mentioned the important role of the chapel staff or the adviser of a religious organization. House mothers and other staff members resident in student dormitories carry weight with students. Some of the warmest expressions of gratitude for help were called forth by occasions which might not normally be thought of as counseling at all—seminars or club meetings at a professor's home, a meal with an assistant dean in the college dining room, or an after-class meeting to ask an academic question which branched out into a revealing discussion of fraternity problems. The college must still be asked whether it wishes to depend on casual contact to serve the guidance function. Can counseling be left to chance?

Religion and religious counselors

Freshmen assigned considerable importance to the presence and activity of religious groups, religious counselors, and nonsectarian or interfaith organizations. Popular opinion holds that college attendance may undermine faith and ethical standards. On the contrary, a number of students feel that seeking out a congenial organization on campus has helped to define their religious position and increase their consciousness of the importance of participation. The responses of students from colleges with church affiliations more frequently mention religious influences than do those of other freshmen, but this seems to be a natural result of the overt encouragement given by the college to religious activities. The individual statements setting high value on religious and ethical counseling seem to be just as convincing whether they emanate from church colleges or not.

Students as counselors

Friends at college appear to be the most important source of help to their classmates, leading by an overwhelming margin any other group identified. Fraternity brothers and sorority sisters, roommates, dormitory companions, any and all of the people to whom the freshman feels close enough to talk frankly, are sought out. The lack of self-consciousness in discussing a problem with a contemporary who is facing, or has recently faced, the same situation far outweighs the chance that an older counselor might be a more expert guide.

Fraternities and sororities encourage their pledges and new members to use the house as a home in this sense, as a source of help in development. More direct molding of the freshman into the "ideal" of the society also occurs, and a few new members echoed one student's comment that he "still tried to be independent and solve his problems himself." This student was discussing his desire to keep friendships he had made before joining a fraternity, even though the friends had joined elsewhere or remained "barbarians." His was one of the few critical remarks directed at fraternities in this connection; most students stressed the desire to discuss their problems with a group in which they felt that their status was secure.

Some unusual notes on student advice appear. One boy reports that his major source of help has been "roommates and friends and a small seminar six of us have organized expressly for the purpose of talking over problems. We're all quite uninhibited and as a result get much done." A girl notes that the campus is so friendly she wouldn't hesitate to talk to almost anyone—"even upperclassmen." A good-sized "bull session" can even afford some anonymity to the questioners. "You can often add a note onto someone's comment without people realizing you're talking about yourself."

The fact that the advice given by other students seems acceptable to the freshman is not necessarily an indication that it is sound or mature. Many people who have problems experience a relief from their tensions as soon as they accept direction from someone else, but this is no assurance that the guidance is wise.

Upperclassmen in the guidance program

Upperclass dormitory advisers, a "big-sister" program or its equivalent, and other provisions made directly by the colleges represent an attempt to make use of this natural tendency for students to help each other, and an attempt to improve the caliber of the advice by selecting some of the advisers. The dean of one college that has developed this plan most fully describes the duties of those participating in the residence program:

In each freshman hall, two hall advisers (upperclass students chosen from interested groups) are assigned to help with the orientation and assimilation of freshmen for the first year. . . . Since hall advisers are peers, more or less, and have no disciplinary function, they can establish firm relations with new students and offer more help to freshmen in relating to other students.

Another dean speaks of the somewhat similar functions of resident student counselors whose duties are even more closely allied to the responsibilities of the faculty counselors:

In addition [to adult Heads of Houses] each house has two Junior Counselors who live in the house during the first semester. These girls are carefully chosen from among the campus leaders and are always strong students and outstanding girls. The Counselors give much time to helping the girls adjust themselves to college life. Since they live with the freshmen, they know each girl very well, and take a sincere interest in her problems. The Counselors confer regularly with the Head of House and with the Deans. . . . Junior Counselors are paid for their services.

In a men's college, there is a student resident program using responsible juniors and seniors in much the fashion described in the statements above. In addition, the college has a full-fledged program using older students for the orientation of resident and nonresident students alike.

At entrance, each freshman is assigned to a student adviser who is a specially selected junior or senior, whose personal character and academic standing are satisfactory, and who has indicated an interest in taking part in the program. No student adviser has more than ten advisees. The student adviser meets his advisees as a group within the first two days of Freshman Week and at this meeting makes arrangements to see each one individually during the rest of the week. Student advisers are especially concerned with adjustment to campus life, but also assist the freshman in reaching an understanding of academic regulations.

As a group, student advisers this past year have done an excellent job. The program is only in its second year, and the improvement this year over last year was noteworthy. The relationship between student advisers and faculty counselors has been excellent throughout, the counselors feeling generally that the student advisers helped the freshmen in the academic as well as in the extracurricular areas. Among the specific improvements due largely to the student advisory program, we believe, is the fact that freshmen seem to find their way to a balanced participation in extracurricular activities more quickly than in previous years.

Guidance apart from the college

Often students go back to those persons who helped them before college. Women, as a group, are more likely to turn to their parents as a source of advice on adjustment problems than are men. It may be pertinent to recall, in this connection, that more women than men in this freshman group came from families in which one or both parents attended college. There may, of course, also be other factors in upbringing or personality which produce this reaction.

Former teachers, friends attending other colleges—especially if they are older—and ministers, physicians, and older relatives also advise the new student. Like the search for advisers among fellow students, the decision to seek out an older person seems to depend not only on qualifications of experience and insight but on the freshman's feeling that he can ask for aid without losing the esteem of the adviser.

The struggle for independence

Certain freshmen carry their determination to stand alone to the point where they prefer not to ask advice from anyone. "Except for academic problems which need immediate solving, I prefer to keep my problems to myself," says one girl. A boy extends this policy even to academic questions. He notes: "I have invariably made all decisions myself this year. When I went to the adviser it was merely to get written approval for my decision so I could act on it." Another boy reports a distinct feeling on his campus that only a weakling seeks advice. "But isn't willingness to seek help a sign of maturity?" he asks.

Only those acquainted with the individual students could know the various reasons for stress on entire self-dependence. Some freshmen imply that it is their duty to learn by their own mistakes and bear their own burdens; others feel that they have escaped serious problems and can handle minor ones without difficulty; a third group seems more defensive about its policy and reiterates the feeling that "it's none of the college's business." A guidance worker might be particularly interested in this third group. There are indications that it includes a proportion of students who may actually be facing considerable difficulties in adjusting to college and to themselves. If, in fact, such students are isolating themselves not only from potential college services but also from the companionship of their classmates, they may be in serious need of the guidance they avoid. One of the deans mentions such a student: "[She] badly wanted directions to resent, and resented not getting them. . . . Her real problem is to achieve the ability to respond positively—her desire for, and antagonism toward, authority is exceptional." Another student is described as "still too frightened to face the need for help."

The central value of guidance

Much more needs to be said about attaining good adjustment in the first year of college. Emphasis on the negative side, on avoiding difficulties and problems, can at best be justified only if it clears the way for positive achievement.

The college is here to guide, and it must not abdicate to the student. If there is any truth in the belief that higher education can be attained more readily, and have more validity, if it comes through the college than if it is left to the chance of individual experience out of school, the college must demonstrate this fact. Guidance is more than a remedy; it is a force with a direction, and this part of college activity, like the academic program itself, must be presented to the student so that its educational meaning is inescapable.

SIX

Introduction to a New College

I

THE RESEMBLANCE between today's colleges and those of a generation ago is deceptive in many important respects. Freshmen have always been "green." But if the modern freshman appears even more hesitant, more confused than his traditional counterpart, it may be because he is entering college with notions about his *alma mater* which are several decades out of date, if they ever corresponded to fact.

First among the changes which have affected modern campuses is size. The growth in American colleges is such that in 1955 almost two and one-half times as many students attended as enrolled in 1930. The size of the current group, which totals between two and three million, has proved both a challenge and a burden. There has been a small increase in the number of colleges, but most of the increased numbers of students have gone to make small colleges larger and large universities greatly larger. The challenge which accompanies the growth has made itself apparent in several ways.

With larger numbers to teach, the colleges are able to offer an increased number of courses and a wider variety of fields of specialization. If, in 1930, only a few students wished to specialize in electronics engineering, or child psychology, or Oriental affairs, and if these students were scattered in several colleges, the chances were poor that they could find sufficient courses in any one place to prepare them adequately. As enrollments have increased, however, the prospective candidate for a degree in a relatively new field has had an increasing number of choices open to him. More colleges have had sufficient demand for courses in new fields, and larger college departments have meant a chance to build up more adequate "majors."

These increases in student populations and college offerings are important parts of the scene to which today's freshmen must adjust. "There are so many majors with requirements and prerequisites that any 'elective system' here is mostly on paper," says one student. Another remarks, "Most courses are so overcrowded that you are lost. Fortunately my major (music) requires some individual attention, so I don't just feel like a cog in a machine."

What is happening to college?

Educational literature of the past quarter century is full of controversy about other effects of the rise in enrollment. Increasing numbers seemed to mean a wider variation in the capacity of students to do what had been considered "standard" academic work, and a wider range in the adequacy of their preparation, as high schools which used to send only a small handful of graduates to college now sent dozens. If the *proportion* of students with lower ability and poor preparation had not changed, at least the sheer numbers of such students had grown. Changing interests increased the demands on the curriculum. Critics inside and outside the colleges asked such awkward questions as: "Aren't the standards of college work being lowered beyond all recognition?" "What are we trying to run, a college or an educational cafeteria?" "What is *college material*? Are we supposed to admit everybody?"

Educators are still searching for answers. Even now, however, new trends indicate that the colleges are already making adjustments. Some of these trends are in fact responsible for the different face on college education—that unfamiliar guise which has surprised many students.

Expanded academic requirements

Most colleges respect the traditional concepts of freshman preparation for the liberal arts or the sciences. They retain requirements—usually a course in English, one leading to a "working knowledge" of the foreign language started in secondary school, a course in mathematics, and one in either the social or physical sciences, or both.

But significant changes have occurred in their curricula, even though the framework of tradition remains, because of the greatly increased numbers of specialties offered. The multiplication is such that one university now offers seven or eight engineering curricula in place of only three a few decades ago. The same increase has taken place in other fields, as the freshmen point out. Each "major" that is added has its own set of prerequisites, and preparing for advanced work engulfs most of the choices the freshman might have beyond the general requirements. In one college, the student in one of the most popular curricula has two elective courses during his freshman year, and no more elective hours until the last half of his senior year.

Since the number of fields of concentration has increased, and since the needs of modern technology have made each one more specialized, there is a great deal of pressure for students to decide on entrance to college what their major fields will be. Early selection of a major demands a degree of certainty about vocational and educational aims which is rarely found among young people. It also cuts deep into the concept of the first year or so of college as a time for exploration and broadening of interest and of knowledge.

The student determines his own course

Those colleges which *require* no specific courses from any freshman, leaving the selection of work to the student, make as rigorous demands on the maturity of the freshman as are made when he must immediately select a major.

The freshman, with his counselor, must examine as well as he can what he wishes to get from college, and where he wishes to aim now and later. Together they must decide what fields he needs to explore further, and ultimately decide where exploration should end and deeper study in a narrower range should begin. The college asks only that the proposed course should make sense in terms of the student involved—his immediate interests and ultimate goals—but this may be an awkward criterion to meet. In these colleges the student and his advisers need an unparalleled amount of information about the freshman's interest, abilities, and shortcomings, if the individually tailored college career is to have real integrity.

While some freshmen prosper under this system of self-determination and responsibility, others feel that there is a lack of definition about a college course conceived in this fashion. At least one freshman in this study granted that her college was making a genuine and challenging attempt to have her take the lead in her educational planning, but she concluded that she would be "happier in a traditional liberal arts course where she knew what was required of her." This student had decided to transfer to such a college for the next year.

The search for a common foundation

In other colleges, the replanning of the freshman year is part of an attempt to redefine, for the present day, the function and content of higher education. Most faculties working on the establishment of such programs assume that college has a general meaning for all students regardless of the choices they eventually make for their major fields, professions, and so on. Some of these colleges, deciding that certain fundamental ideas appearing in the ancient or contemporary world are of strategic importance for the educated man or woman today, have set up courses in which the basic sources are drawn from several areas—sciences, the humanities, the arts, and literature. Other courses maintain traditional subjects or disciplines, but provide opportunities for students and teachers to recognize the relations between ideas in one field and those of another.

On some campuses, these so-called "general courses" take up only part of the student's time. In others, they involve most of the work of both the first and second years. The technical college, or one with some other professional specialty such as teacher training, sometimes counts on the basic course to provide the "common denominator" of education for "the rest of living"; that is, to educate the future specialist in his responsibilities as a citizen, in his obligations as a cultivated person, or in his opportunities to serve his community outside of his chosen work. In still other colleges, stress is on methods of criticism and thinking which may have validity for all fields.

An overview of the programs

These illustrations only begin to describe three significant ways the colleges have tried to meet the new era. The first method is the most direct outgrowth of the older college. It posits certain basic courses, prescribed from a long-term observation of the needs of students who wish to go on to specialized curricula. It responds to the modern need for more and more intensive training by increasing the number of majors offered, and requires the freshman to make early selections among the majors so that he may take the first steps in his training as soon as possible. The second type of program turns its back on generalizations about education in order to face the question of individual needs and clear the way for individual decisions about college and the student's future. It states, at least by implication, that no educational plan has validity for all students, but that abilities and objectives differ so much and so significantly that a different course of study for each one may be necessary and desirable. The third approach to education envisions a possible common foundation for all students, so that all may communicate regardless of specialty.

There is probably no college that falls neatly into any one of the categories, so far as its solution to the major questions of freshman courses is concerned. Some colleges have offered experimental courses to only part of the enrollment, others report that highly original approaches to teaching and learning are undertaken by a few departments, but that the remainder are untouched. Yet the ferment is there, and freshmen as well as faculties must deal with its results.

II

A broader base for college "education"

The growth in self-examination at college has gone far beyond the realm of the academic program. What has happened is nothing less than the rise of the concept that whatever happens to the student during college is "educational" in the sense that education is the training and guided development of the whole person. The faculty is not the only educational force at work on the student, but it may be one of the few exercising conscious or intentional influence on him. Consequently, it cannot afford to act thoughtlessly, or to let a poor decision in one area handicap what is undertaken in another.

The freshman who said the continual hazing at his college made him so mad all day he didn't care if he studied at night; the girl who wouldn't keep appointments with her college adviser because the advisers in high school had dispensed school discipline rather than counsel on educational problems; the student who refused to write a term paper because he felt his professor questioned the wisdom of a policy of his church; all these are educational casualties. Most colleges would see them as such. But where to draw the line between guidance and unwarranted interference, or between encouraging self-reliance and failing to correct a potentially dangerous situation is an individual matter with each institution. Most faculties believe, however, that it must be a matter of decision and intelligent attention, not a matter of inertia and indifference.

Aim: the right college for the student

In their reports on adjusting to college, the freshmen traced some of their problems to difficulties in selecting a college. To the college, the student's query, "Did I choose the right college?" implies another, "Did we admit the right students?" Students can, as they have shown, select unwisely because of undue emphasis on the reputation of a college, because of some peripheral aspect of college life like athletic standing, or because of misconceptions about the academic program. Colleges have been known to select unwisely, too. Leaving aside what might be called questionable practices, such as recruiting for athletes, even some "respectable" or attractive selection method like requiring high scholastic standing may mislead a faculty about the quality of its students.

Colleges have suffered in times when few students applied for entrance because selection was not economically feasible. They have also suffered when large numbers of candidates had to be evaluated, because of the mechanical application of criteria like high test scores or a certain rank in the high school class. Few colleges have been so unfortunate as to admit only students who are too intelligent! However, some colleges have discovered that students with high academic records can have serious personal maladjustments. In such cases, the college must be prepared to deal with the student's handicapped personal life, or admit that it has failed to select wisely.

In fact, the wide variety of college programs today is a tremendous resource for the high school counselor and his charges. It is almost true that there is a rewarding college experience available to any high school graduate. And, given a college consonant with the educational and personal aims of the student, sound training can result. Many features may contribute directly to the ultimate adjustment of the student: availability of work in the student's field of interest, size, religious affiliation, expense of attending, scholarship or employment opportunities, and a host of others. It is no coincidence that these qualities are among those identified by the freshmen as sources of difficulty as well. The point is that if certain circumstances are worthy of consideration after the student has entered, they are worth study beforehand, for their effect on the mutual selection of student and college.

Can the university assume a new role?

State universities and other institutions required by law to accept any graduate of an accredited high school in the state protest from time to time that selection is all very well for the small private college, but can have no part in their thinking. There are signs that this self-defeating attitude may change, as these universities work more closely with the secondary schools, and as counselors become increasingly aware of the experience of their local graduates at the university. Some of the "guidance by elimination"—that is, wholesale weeding out of freshmen who do not succeed—does harm to the individuals who fail, and adds a considerable financial burden to the state. There are as yet few educators who suggest that the publicly supported universities should refuse entrance to large groups of students. There are many, however, who urge that candidates for entrance should understand the type of competition they may find at the college, the standards of work required for continuance on the rolls, and the chances of success for students who had only average grades in high school.

Building up better secondary school guidance and thereby helping the student know the contemporary college better may not make headlines for a college. Yet, in the long view, the same urge which produces a new general education theory may produce a new recognition of the vital need to avoid mistakes in admitting students. Whether or not a college can refuse admissions, it still has, like the most exclusive school, an obligation to see that those who come do so with their eyes open.

III

Orientation to college

The "shake-down cruise" of the Navy has its parallel in college. "Freshman week," or "orientation week," as it is variously called, is already a tradition, and characterizes the period at the beginning of the year when both college and newcomer are concerned with getting off to a good start. Typically, this is a period before classes begin, during which a tremendous amount of information is poured into the freshman and some additional information is secured from him, and at the end of which he is presumably ready to function as a *student*, all lesser matters having been left behind.

Use of the orientation period for academic counseling and placement testing has already been mentioned. Faculty and upperclassmen also introduce the freshman to the program of activities, the geography of campus and town, and the spiritual, recreational, and cultural selections open to him. The social is mingled with the academic reception, and freshmen report that the experience is usually enjoyable except for the crowded calendar of events. Some freshmen plead that some of the demands—particularly for settling down to take tests and make course selections—should proceed at a slower pace.

The growth and refinement of concepts of orientation is a striking development of the recent decades. Many of the changes aim at giving the student greater freedom for self-direction and seeing that he has sufficient information about the college and about himself so that *his* decisions will be sound ones.

A year of orientation

Several programs supplement the brief orientation period by meetings held throughout the year. One of the most fully developed has been introduced at a college which arranges for many students to do exploratory work in regular jobs outside the college in semesters alternating their periods of full-time study. Others carry jobs on campus along with their studies.

The weekly orientation sessions, which are organized for each dormitory group, stress three important areas of adjustment. The first acquaints the student more fully with the meaning of membership in the college community, dealing with how to live in a dormitory, how to make the most of campus facilities and activities, and how community standards are cooperatively established and maintained. A second major undertaking of the orientation seminars is to provide skilled help in planning for work and study. Specialists from the college personnel offices discuss the evaluation and improvement of reading and study techniques. A third focus is on the individual's determination of his educational aims. He writes a paper exploring the relation of his objectives to what he expects to do in college and in the work program. Those students who are participating in the off-campus work program, as the dean of the college points out, "carry out their own responsibilities as anyone working." The college assumes a dual role in preparing freshmen for the initial work term and in helping the student assimilate the experience derived from employment into the rest of his education. Provision is made for research in occupational selection and preparation.

Basic skills for college

Orientation of the student is not the whole story. It may be necessary, all too often, to orient the faculty as well. If students come to college with ideas about what to expect which are out-of-date and out-of-focus, teachers also may face freshman classes with stereotyped notions of their preparation and readiness.

Deans complain that an inexperienced faculty member may try to teach freshmen as if *they* should start where *his* graduate work left off. His enthusiasm for the higher branches of his subject may blind him to the need of starting *where the freshman is.*

A favorite college administrative pastime has been sniping at the secondary school—saying that graduates are unprepared for sustained effort and low in fundamental reading, writing, and study skills. High schools retort that the colleges are largely responsible for entrance requirements written in terms of specific subjects, and that it would greatly strengthen their hand if colleges were to shift to greater stress on learning capacities.

There is no doubt that there is wide variation in almost any freshman group—even the most highly selected—in individual level of reading and work skills, such as English usage, writing fluency, and so on. There is no perfect correlation between the presence of these skills and high ability. As numbers of freshmen increase, the opportunity of the college to do something about the situation by economical group methods increases too, since the actual number of students to be helped is sufficient to make special provisions for them worth while.

Existing college programs in the skills

Thinking about variations in terms of opportunity for upgrading has already been productive. A good many college programs could be cited, but one established at a school *without* a selective admissions policy seems particularly promising. This college conducts its courses and laboratory work in skills improvement as part of a general division for the guidance and placement of students before major curricula are designated. The exploratory character of this division provides a natural setting for the study of reading level, reading speed, study and library techniques, report writing, and other working skills. Both group techniques and individual work with reading specialists are offered.

Another college, with a rather highly selected student body, provides courses which may be attended either by students with marked weaknesses or students who are working at a high level but nevertheless realize that an honors program, or graduate work in the offing, make still greater improvement desirable. These courses tackle reading and study skills in a broader setting. Their approach is based on the concept that a student needs, in addition, practice and training in learning how to concentrate, how to schedule study by day and week, how to take notes on readings and lectures, how to take tests, how to appraise his own academic strengths and weaknesses, and how to get along with teachers and fellow students. As the director of the program states, "To be more 'educable,' a student must develop all of the above traits within his capacity. Although he may believe that he has acquired all but one desirable academic trait, he cannot effectively reshape his academic personality by attempting to master the absent trait alone—any more than a successful runner can train himself to become a baseball pitcher merely by exercising his right arm."

Desire for excellence

When colleges adopt a positive attitude toward starting with the student *where he is,* they assume responsibility for the able as well as for the less able. Possibly thinking about the able student as "gifted" is not much more useful than placing the stigma "remedial" on the attempt to help the student in the lower part of the range. An astute psychologist has pointed out that we are all "handicapped" in terms of our own ideals. An attack on the problems of all students admitted should not be beneath the dignity of any college. If reading skills seem inadequate, they may be so because college work calls on skills never before needed, or skills which did not need to be developed at so high a level. There is nothing unhealthy in this situation. A college worth its charter can only welcome the opportunity to ask for more and better work, to place the ceiling on performance high, and to help and stimulate the student to attain levels he did not before imagine.

Progression in skills should be matched by progression in thinking, at least according to the aspirations of most faculties. Students, too, demand that it should be so, and in the name of this objective ask to proceed onward from high school without a backward step, and ask for practice in "the kind of thinking demanded at college," even before entrance. When such thinking should be introduced—grade nine, or eleven, or twelve—must wait upon further investigation.

IV

There is no substitute for education

If successful adjustment to college has any meaning, then, it must promote growth in educational stature. So long as orientation was regarded as largely preventive—seeking to avoid per-

sonal difficulty and to clear up preliminary academic problems—
it was all too easy for the college to go on believing that "education" was a matter for the faculty, while "guidance" was a matter
for the deans and counselors. Just as the selection problem
changed with the acceptance of the "admission of the whole
person," so the teaching problem can change when it is recognized
that the "whole college" bears on the student. Certain efforts
have been made to explore this proposition as it affects students
of high standing.

At least one experimental program with superior students is
unusual in its combined attack on student needs for stable personal guidance, for close personal relations with both classmates
and faculty, and for integration within the program of studies
itself. The first aim is provided for by the assignment of a single
adviser to a segment of the freshman class which is regarded as
both a counseling and an academic unit. The adviser knows the
students through individual conference and also as a group. This
same group moves, again as a unit, into two sets of freshman
courses—usually in English and social science. The faculty conducting the courses has a partner in the adviser, "instead of
getting piecemeal information from several counselors in as many
conferences as there are advisers involved." The courses to which
the group goes have two unusual features. They are two-course
sequences taught by the same faculty member, and they are, by
plan, integrated with each other. Thus what is presented as both
a basic and cultural course in English and literature is related
to work in contemporary civilization and the social sciences.

Further study of this particular experiment has led to establishing a more unified curriculum for the first two years of college, both within and outside the pattern of sequence courses,
and for other groups as well as those in the experiment. Related
to progress in curriculum planning is more adjustment to individual differences and to developing the capacity for inde-

pendent study. By crediting guided work in independent reading, prescribed courses can be fulfilled without class attendance. Qualified students are permitted to move rapidly into advanced courses.

The Experimental Program serves in many ways to assist the student in the difficult period of transition between high school and college. His academic and personal needs are diagnosed and cognizance is taken of his problems; then such measures are provided as will best enable him to adjust satisfactorily to a new type of life and community. Most significantly, however, he is treated as a responsible human being, one who, no longer carefully supervised every step of the way, initiates his own special projects and independently carries them through to fruition in a manner consonant with the intellectual judgment and maturity which he has achieved as a result of guidance and training furnished him by the College.

When are they ready for college?

College has traditionally followed four years of high school, and "college age" has traditionally been from eighteen to twenty-one years. Yet such rigorous classifications run counter to the known variations in growth and development of individuals. The experience of high schools and colleges with veterans whose formal education had been interrupted did much to familiarize teachers with the effects of lapse of time on retention of skills and knowledge, and also brought out some of the advantages of the mature student. Never again, perhaps, will there be quite the same easy generalization about "the right time for college." At the other end of the scale, the desire to accelerate admission of students to college because of the imminence of the draft into military service has recently given schoolmen some experience with evaluating younger students whose preparation had been compressed into less than the usual four calendar years.

The outstanding experiment in lowering the age of college entrance has been the Program of Early Admission to College, sponsored by the Fund for the Advancement of Education, established by the Ford Foundation.[1] The program studied the experience of groups of superior students, mostly under 16½ years of age and the majority of whom had completed only the tenth or eleventh grade of secondary school. Exploration of the effects of early admission has been concerned not only with the academic records of the groups but also with their social and emotional adjustment. The younger groups were carefully selected for qualities of ability and maturity, and study of both college and post-college success are under way.

This study is a cooperative undertaking, involving as it does not only a dozen colleges and a great many preparatory schools, both public and private, but also the Educational Testing Service, which is conducting the evaluation program. Implicitly, the experiment involves even larger numbers, since part of the study procedure requires the evaluation, for comparative purposes, of groups of students of the same level of aptitude who completed high school and entered college at the usual age. The tentative conclusions reached on the basis of the first groups and their progress are favorable on all counts—academic records, social and personal adjustment, and continuation in college.

Acceleration and enrichment

Saving time for the student is only one aim of acceleration programs—saving his enthusiasm for learning, avoiding the repetition in college of work already done in high school, and establishing more genuine integration of the education he receives in both institutions are even more significant objectives. Moreover, lessons learned by educators planning the work at both levels can have great importance for other students.

Other studies sponsored by the Fund for the Advancement

[1] A more complete description of the several experimental programs conducted by the Foundation is given in *Bridging the Gap Between School and College* (New York: The Fund for the Advancement of Education, 1953).

of Education have had an influence on educational theory far beyond what might be expected from the relatively small groups of *students* so far affected. Reference has already been made to various exploratory curricula linked by a concern with general education. One of the best known projects, under the Fund, has been that conducted by faculty members of three boys' preparatory schools—Andover, Exeter, and Lawrenceville—and three universities—Harvard, Princeton, and Yale. This project had integration of grades eleven through fourteen specifically in mind, in an effort, on the one hand, to avoid repeating courses and, on the other, to avoid dropping a subject before it had been pursued long enough for real insights to emerge. Curricular dislocations were not the only ones uncovered, however. Lack of a positive orientation toward general education was pinpointed as a weakness appearing in students, possibly because it appeared also among faculties. If the implications of this study are taken to heart by schools and colleges, it is believed that the best students might shorten the combined school-college program by as much as a year.

The enrichment of the program in the high schools is an objective of two other Fund projects, that associating the public schools of Portland, Oregon, with Reed College, and the more elaborate project known as the School and College Study of Admission with Advanced Standing. Both stress the importance of making all academic work rich and challenging, particularly for the student of unusual capacity or of special endowment in some creative or intellectual field. A Fund report affirms "that sound learning is respectable and that academic subjects, the content of a liberal arts education, constitute worthy intellectual and spiritual nourishment for young minds, if these disciplines are liberally and wisely taught." With such a proposition in mind, the projects deal directly with course content and with definitions of accomplishment—a necessary attention if schools and colleges are to make this enrichment a matter of fact rather than of pious hope.

Experiments confirm student reports

It is interesting to summarize the trends which are illustrated by these experiments. Although one may deal chiefly with curriculum, another with correct placement, a third with orientation, a fourth with acceleration, all bear on the basic problem of integrating the educational experience of the individual.

Moreover, the new studies confirm in a striking way the observations made by the freshmen reporting on their own histories. Selection of a college is crucial. Adjustment in the personal and social areas is related to academic well-being. Guidance and self-reliance are like the obverse and reverse of a medal, both necessary to the student. Above all, individual development must run like a thread through all levels of schooling. Abrupt changes in direction and purpose occurring when the high school career ends and the college career starts are wasteful and harmful.

So long as "transition" from school to college is characterized by only one common element—the same student—freshmen will be crippled by adjustment difficulties and many will be permanently lost to higher education. Today the search is on for other bridges across the gap—a well-thought-out progression in liberal studies in school and college, a guidance system more alert to human beings than merely to "problems," and a social policy that helps the student contribute fully to both high school and college community. Today some of these solutions exist in potential only. The years ahead will show if schoolmen can return as students to their own educational systems, and meet new demands for achievement which, like the freshmen, they never before imagined.

SEVEN

Assignment for Tomorrow

I

AWARENESS of "problems and adjustments," or of "frustrations and satisfactions," is in itself a sign that evaluation is taking place. Freshmen begin to organize their experiences and their responses to experience from the earliest hours at college. However, willingness to suspend judgment is demanded, also. It is wise to wait "until the honeymoon is over," or until the initial shock effect has worn off, before requiring a generalization on which to build. How did these students, in the spring of the freshman year, look at the whole enterprise of being freshmen?

Nearly half agreed that "I have found my freshman year a very satisfactory experience and am enthusiastic about life at this college." In addition, a little over a third were generally satisfied and had no serious criticisms about the way their freshman year had been organized and planned. About one out of five, however, made a final summary which was less favorable. They felt the arrangements should be considerably improved, or even went so far as to agree that the year was "unsatisfactory in several respects which I believe need marked improvement if it is to be a really valuable educational experience."

It was suggested earlier that perhaps freshmen were too close to their own situation, and that juniors or seniors would be able to give a more mature estimate of the significance of being a freshman. Such a claim can be countered by saying that any obstacle successfully surmounted would appear unimportant by the time the security of upperclass years had been reached. It is a sobering thought that, if these 470 freshmen were typical of nationwide trends in enrollment, only about 235 of them would survive as students to graduate from any college. Among *all* freshmen, personal reasons will cause some withdrawals; some men will be called for military service; other students will change their goals and decide that the way toward them does not lead through college. But perhaps half those leaving will go because of scholastic failure, or other reasons connected directly with education at the college level.

That year is immediately important, not only for those who survive or leave but to all concerned with the students or their training. It is easy to say, "they should never have come in the first place"—but they *were* admitted. It is tempting to feel that "college may still have given them something worth while," but the human expense to students, their parents, and the colleges cannot be justified by any such tenuous hope.

In point of fact, since a large proportion of this freshman sample is drawn from selective colleges, one would anticipate a smaller percentage of drop-outs than in the total college population. Students admitted after careful screening are the very ones for whom the greatest success in college would be predicted, since such factors as aptitude, preparation, and personal qualifications have been taken into account in their admission. Yet 20 per cent of the 470 reported serious doubts about the value of their freshman programs. If people in *this* group are dissatisfied, in spite of the care taken to choose them, the methods used for admissions and those applied in guiding and teaching are all thrown into question. Higher education can ill afford to lose one out of five, and it should be unthinkable to continue to lose one out of two.

To whom do they speak?

The challenge of the freshmen must be taken up by a group of weary, over-worked, middle-aged school people. Principals, teachers, admissions officers, deans, and college presidents are fully aware that changes cannot be made in a moment. They see all the inconsistencies and irrelevancies in the complaints of the freshmen, and they know that youthful experience alone cannot guide an enterprise the size of American education. But educators have to be idealists too. They believe that people can be taught.

The lessons the freshmen have set out for the secondary schools and colleges will occupy most of the space in the following pages. At the end, however, is a section for students; for both the educators and the freshmen realize that they share between them the responsibility for the future.

II

What do the freshmen say to their schools?

Secondary schools exist in such variety, differ so much in the policies of dealing with college preparatory students, and are so widely separated in the success with which they accomplish their goals that what might be said of one would have no pertinence at all for another. The following attempts to generalize may not fit perfectly into the needs and demands of any one school. However, the brief student comments which follow the recommendations make clear the intent of the request and indicate the student need on which it is based.

Regarding the educational program

1. *Provide a sound educational program for all students* based on a consideration of pupil needs and abilities as well as on the special requirements faced by college-bound students. "I came from a small school. Only three others in my class went to college, so there was no special attention to our needs except emphasis on marks. My principal didn't even know what the College Boards were." "Fortunately, I came from an independent school with an excellent reputation for college preparation. I feel that I have had a much broader education than some of the other freshmen." "I went to a school with very rigid requirements—four years of Latin, three of math, etc. Now, I have no idea how to face 'general education' courses."

2. *Give more weight to training in techniques for college work,* including study skills, reading, use of the library, ability to write well, to organize ideas, to adjust to special procedures such as lectures or laboratory work, and to carry out long-term assignments without constant supervision. "I never learned how to study." "Assignments were so specific the thinking was all done for you." "College work isn't necessarily more difficult, but there's so much of it."

3. *Provide school counselors with adequate training* for pre-college advisement *and allow them ample time* to work with individual pupils about their aims and requirements. The desire of the freshmen for more and better guidance has strong support in studies of the value of counseling. For example, a careful survey of the effect of counseling in secondary school, which was carried on in Wisconsin, indicated that the guided group had a lower average rate of failure than the unguided group, made fewer curriculum changes, and had a higher mean scholastic rating. A significantly larger proportion of the guided group entered college and a larger proportion of those who entered

stayed in college.[1] "The biggest need at our high school is for better counseling." "My school gave to each student all the help and attention needed. This counseling was invaluable." "It's hard to have the personal relationship I spoke of when classes are so large, but if advisors had that goal in mind they would do a lot more good."

Regarding the student himself

4. *Provide the student with adequate, dependable information about his own abilities, progress, and accomplishments* interpreted in the light of his educational and vocational goals. This is closely related to the recommendation on student counseling, for unless this information is in the books of the counselor, and is wisely used by him, it may be useless or even harmful. "I guess it goes back to 'know thyself,' but most of us have no clear idea how our abilities stack up or how well we should expect to do against college competition." "Give vocational interest tests." "Give ability tests *early* enough to do some good. We had no testing earlier than the senior year." "Give several tests. I think there is too much emphasis laid on IQ alone." "I always got good marks, but no one ever discussed *how* good my work ought to be till I took placement tests here."

5. *Secure reliable and extensive information about colleges for the use of students and counselors.*

a. *This information should include entrance requirements, standards of work, and college educational programs.* "If you weren't going to 'State,' my school was no help whatever." "We heard altogether too much about high marks required for entrance, *nothing* about required courses after you got here." "Somehow, give the students an idea of the competition they will face."

---

[1] John W. M. Rothney and Bert A. Roens, *Guidance of American Youth* (Cambridge: Harvard University Press, 1952), pp. 216-17. Also correspondence with Professor Rothney in May 1956.

"My school counselor even helped me choose my freshman courses."

b. *It should also include material on college life in broader terms*—living arrangements, special provisions for the guidance and adjustment of freshmen, the freedom and restrictions of the campus, and other factors contributing to the social and personal growth of students. "Everybody stressed how friendly the place was, but not how isolated." "No Middle Westerner should ever come here to college." "We had far more freedom in high school than I have here."

6. *Arrange for firsthand contact of students with college representatives, graduates now in college, and other persons in close touch with college programs.* Many colleges will, if requested, send a representative to a school to give information and answer the questions of possible applicants. "My school even arranged for us to visit several colleges." "I came from so far away, I had to depend on pictures, but one teacher who had visited this campus helped a lot." "I wish I could have talked to a freshman here. Somehow, information given this way would have impressed me more than having a teacher tell me the same thing."

7. *Stress the value of school and community activities as preparation for college,* insofar as these provide "practice in responsibility," purposeful cooperation with contemporaries and adults, and contact with people outside the pupil's immediate circle. "Working in our church service group was the most valuable thing I ever did." "I had worked in all sorts of jobs, in summers, and found I was much more mature than many of my classmates because of this." "Somehow I should have been made to realize there were so many types of people in college."

In school and college relations

8. *Know the students well and see that the college is given information on the personal characteristics as well as the ability*

and achievement of applicants and admitted freshmen. Information about personal characteristics should not be based on opinions drafted in haste at the end of the high school course. It should be a consensus compiled over the secondary school years from school records that provide a continuous study and report of salient facts about each student.

9. *Request follow-up information from colleges on both the academic records and personal adjustment of graduates of the school.* "Everybody I know who went on to college has had this trouble in English." "I think my high school does a very good job preparing for academic studies, but it should teach us how to become progressively more independent each year." "I feel that improvement should start in the high school—in academic and social problems, both. I think the college is doing an excellent job—considering what the high schools have done."

10. *Work closely and continuously with colleges to secure a better articulation of the educational programs of secondary school and college.* "I definitely feel the high school could include the first two years of college work." "What you did in high school seems to have nothing to do with what goes on in college. There is not so much a transition as a regression and repetition."

III

What is the message for the colleges?

The freshmen felt that most of their adjustment problems had to be solved at college. Some of them could scarcely be anticipated by the high school. But many problems encountered by the students had their roots as far back as the initial decision to prepare for college and the steps taken to select a college, so the suggestions to the colleges include improvement of communications with the high school. Other recommendations are directed at orientation and the steps taken to introduce freshmen to life at college. Finally, the college is encouraged to define its own position in the educational scheme, for the benefit of the college itself, its patrons and friends, the high schools, and the student body.

Selection and admission, a job for school and college

In admitting students, regardless of whether or not the college can apply selection standards, the students urge that the colleges

1. *Use every possible means to inform prospective students and their schools about the academic, social, and cultural life of the campus.* "Catalogs shouldn't be expected to 'sell' the student on the college as well as tell him about courses, schedules, and degrees." "I am sure there must be good middle western and far western colleges, but no one seemed to have information about them." "College Night was a big help, but how can you select a college at the last minute?"

2. *Establish and maintain close contacts with the schools preparing applicants* so that records of both academic and personal growth can be adequately interpreted for the improvement of admission procedures. "If my father and our minister hadn't been to college, I'd never have gone. There certainly was no encouragement in school or our rural town to think about more education." "Someone should help the school counselors to face the fact that 50 per cent of the freshmen at this college drop out." "If my school is going to teach chemistry and physics, it should learn what colleges think about modern methods. The way it was taught and the book used seem to be the very thing that intelligent liberal arts teachers are fighting—useless memorized facts."

3. *Study entrance requirements carefully in the light of both subject matter preparation and the basic skills, attitudes, and abilities needed for success in college work.* There is much evidence that the study of particular subjects is of less importance (except as they are prerequisites for certain courses) than the develop-

ment of work habits and skills. The college's statement of its requirements might therefore well emphasize the basic skills needed for its work and so encourage the school to give greater attention to these. "Getting into this college is no problem. Getting anything out of it unless you have darned good preparation is another matter." "Some way should be found to convince high school students that learning to study as deeply as you can into a subject is the biggest part of preparation."

After the student enters

The first days of the college year may be far too late in the process to effect the real introduction of the student to the educational program. Much is actually done by some colleges between acceptance and entrance, so that one girl reports, "It seemed as if I got mail from the college once a week all summer. Discussion of freshman courses which I was to go over with my school adviser came before school closed. Then there were letters from the housing committee, my 'big sister,' and by the time I arrived I felt I knew the college and was already known there."

Recommendations for the thorough orientation of the freshmen stress the need of the student to feel a part of a living community. In this connection, the students advise that a college should:

4. *Make a real effort to make the student a partner in the educational program.* "Participating in an experimental curriculum really is a wonderful experience." "They used to tell us in school 'take this because you'll need it later.' Now we *know* why courses are required for the basic arts program, etc." "I feel that we should have broader areas to choose our courses from, and specifications somewhat gripe me—but I see what they're driving at."

5. *Adopt a basic philosophy of guidance,* providing for the needs of individual students, and accepting individual differences

in ability, interests, and achievement as a part of the responsibility to provide, so far as possible, a meaningful education for each. "I have used the counseling services fully and often, especially because no one tells you what to do. Instead they help you explore yourself, your own interests, and so on, and then explain what the college has that will help toward your goals." "I sometimes wish we had requirements, because making all your own decisions is hard work. But on vacation when I met classmates who had gone to other colleges, I realized how much I had grown up because of the emphasis on independence." "I came from a large high school and am amazed at the interest individual faculty and deans here take in each student's progress."

6. *Encourage, by every means available, the full use of the college counseling services for freshmen.* "We have a placement officer, but I wouldn't know where to find her or what to say if I did." "Counseling is available to whatever extent the student wants to use it—very large or very small." "I think the college should place even more stress on the religious counselors available."

7. *Devote time and attention to expanded guidance services,* including facilities for educational diagnosis and remediation, psychological services, and vocational guidance. "Our academic advisers have had much help because we have a trained psychologist and a vocational guidance specialist available." "The college offers a study course, followed if you wish by a course in reading. I have found these a big help." "There is a great deal of activity centered around the use of our free term for exploring vocations."

8. *Give careful consideration to the assignment of faculty members to freshman courses,* in the light of the extensive comments made about adequacy of instruction and the importance of faculty attitudes. Students stress the significance of these factors for maintaining a high quality of interest and stimulation, as well as aca-

demic soundness, in freshman work. "I find college just like high school in this area. If a course is well taught you work hard and respect the course and the teacher."

9. *Examine and evaluate the educational effect of policies concerning the community life of the college.* This involves assessing policies about the relation of curriculum and cocurriculum, the place of fraternities and sororities, the social values in arrangements for housing, meals, recreation, and so forth, the role of the chapel and religious programs, and the improvement of student-faculty relations. This recommendation is related to the guidance philosophy and the counseling program of the institution. "There are so many worthwhile activities going on that budgeting time becomes a major problem." "Life in a fraternity has a way of affecting your attitudes toward study, sports, and activities as well as your social life."

10. *Give further attention to the orientation program in the light of promising experiments now under way in some colleges.* The college's responsibility goes beyond the intellectual one. Its students are still in the formative period, and their development in character and in social adjustment will be vitally affected by their life on the campus. "The system of upperclass counselors is a great help." "Perhaps the use of 'big sisters' should last beyond Freshman Week." "A great deal of stress is put on the study of your own values in adjusting to other students and the college."

The college and its educational obligations

The world of the college includes more than its students, of course. The college of today may act as a research institute for industry or the government. The public obligations of the state-supported university may range from agricultural economics to crime detection. The college also has a home in the town or city that surrounds it. "Town and gown" relations have a great effect on the life of the student, and may help him define his eventual role as a citizen in his own community. The college is supported, financially but above all spiritually, by those who understand it. Even freshmen are aware that they and their parents, just as truly as wealthy benefactors, are patrons of the college. This network of influence and support exists because the college is an *educational* force. Its definition of itself in relation to the growth and development of youth makes up the character of the college, and this character will in the final analysis determine the role of the college in all its other contacts with society.

From this background rises the final recommendation to the college.

11. *The college should work closely with secondary schools, students, and other groups to study the educational needs of young people and the part the college can best take in serving these needs. It should make every effort to improve the articulation between school and college so that education shall be a continuous process of growth for each student. In so doing, each college should furnish for its own students the opportunity to pursue a sound education conceived in relation to the goals which the college accepts for itself.*

IV

For students only

Freshmen take themselves and their problems seriously. Out of all their personal and unique reports come lessons for their schools and colleges that will be important for years to come. But the emphasis of the students is rightly on *themselves, their* problems, and *their* solutions. So, to the freshmen of the next years, these students give the hardest assignments of all: know yourself. Know where you are going and how the college can help you on your way.

1. *Early in your high school career begin planning whether to*

attend college. Take time to learn about entrance requirements, to consider colleges of different types, and finally to select the colleges where you wish to apply. The process should take at least two years, perhaps longer.

2. *Study yourself first.* Secure and use all the information the school can give you on your aptitudes, interests, and scholastic progress. Use this information to set up definite educational aims and at least tentative or general vocational goals.

3. *Recognize the importance of sound high school work* as a preparation for sound college work. Do not expect to loaf through school and then turn over a new leaf when you get to college.

4. *There is more to preparation than what you do in school.* The freshmen who adjust most easily are those who have had experience working with people, in school and out, who are used to accepting responsibility, who have been active in community and church, and who have learned to recognize and adjust to differences in purposes, standards, and personalities without losing sight of their own goals.

5. *Make the fullest possible use of the guidance and advisory services of the school.* Use them both in learning about yourself and in selecting and preparing for a college.

6. *Select colleges on the basis of relevant points.* The educational program will have a greater long-term effect on you than the fact that some old friend started there last year. Finances are crucial but if you choose a college merely because you can afford it you will have to learn to make the best of it. Think first about what sort of college you want, then about the colleges that seem to fit your requirements.

7. *Find out everything possible about the colleges you consider most carefully.* Talk to people who know about the college firsthand. Talk to a student now attending if you can possibly do so. Read *carefully* the materials the college prepares for you. Plan to visit the campus if this can be arranged. Ask as well as answer

questions when you are interviewed for admission. Think about the fact that you will be studying, making friends, rooming, and playing at the college. Inquire about all these sides of campus life. Ask about academic, personal, and religious counseling.

8. *When the big moment arrives, do not let the hectic life confuse you too long.* Recognize that adjusting to college is complicated. Conserve and direct your energies toward adjusting first in the most important areas.

9. *Budget adequate study time from the start.* Once you fall behind you will have trouble straightening out. You will be up against some stiff competition and some high standards. Learn to evaluate both without hesitation.

10. *Study your courses.* Learn what each demands from you in the way of time required, special methods of reading, taking notes, library research, and so on. Tackle weak points in your study procedures just as you would try to make up for a gap in your subject-matter knowledge.

11. *Give the college a chance to furnish helpful guidance for adjustment.* Know what resources the college offers and take advantage of them. An academic, personal, or vocational problem will probably be of concern to someone on campus besides your roommate. Be independent, but not bullheaded.

12. *Make the most of the college facilities for a full life.* Participate in the cultural and recreational programs, clubs and activities, and the religious programs as often as you can in view of the necessary allotment of time for the academic side. When you look for friends and advisers, remember the faculty is human, too.

13. *Evaluate the activities you enter,* see what you get out of them and what they contribute to your exploration of your interests and abilities. Use this evaluation as a guide to cutting down or increasing your participation.

14. *You will be on your own in many ways,* deciding your own values and standards of conduct, managing your own time and

money, working out your own opinions. This is part of your education. You will get more out of it if you make your choices with your eyes open than if you drift with the crowd. Also, know enough to know when talking it over will help.

15. *Have a plan of action, and know how the college contributes to it.* You are not expected to know all the answers; part of your college education should be exploring the intellectual world. But keep your general objectives in mind and clarify them as you get more information about yourself and the possibilities open to you.

16. *Become a part of your college.* Know what it stands for, in education as well as athletics. Every student who goes to college receives some financial aid, for tuition never pays all the expense. You can best repay your college by making the most of the opportunities it offers, but it is also your responsibility to be constructive and optimistic, and to do whatever you can to make life there rewarding both to yourself and to others.

17. *You are the prime mover in your own education.*

APPENDIX A

The Questionnaire

EDUCATIONAL RECORDS BUREAU
21 Audubon Avenue
New York 32, N.Y.

March, 1954

QUESTIONNAIRE ON TRANSITION FROM SCHOOL TO COLLEGE

You have been chosen as one of a group of freshmen in American colleges who are being asked to contribute your thoughts on problems of adjustment to college life. Most students entering college have certain difficulties arising from conditions that are different from those at home and in secondary school. We plan to summarize your replies and the replies of other freshmen and then to try to work out procedures that will help smooth out these difficulties for future classes.

Please fill in the following blanks:

(You need not sign your name unless you wish to do so; this is intended to be an anonymous questionnaire):

College attended by student reporting————————————
(College will not be identified in report)

Age of student ———— Sex: M ————
                            F ————

Date of graduation from secondary school ————————

Graduate of ————————————————————————
           Name of school and location (*will not be identified in report*)

Approximate number in graduating class ————

127

Public or private school? _____
Location of home:
Large city _____ Medium-sized city _____ Small city _____
Suburb _____ Small town _____ Rural _____
Father's occupation _____
Did father attend college? _____ Did mother attend college? _____
Are there fraternities or sororities on campus? _____
Do you belong to one of them? _____
Student's residence while in college: at home _____ in private home
_____ in rooming house _____ in dormitory _____ fraternity
house _____ sorority house _____ (*Please check*)
Number of roommates _____

General instructions.—In Part I, we have listed some problems that
may be suggestive of certain phases of college experience where you
may have found difficulty. Please place a check mark beside the types
of problems that have given you difficulty. Under "Others" list any
other problems which you feel are important to you as a college
student. You may write brief comments on any of the problems
below the list and on the back of the page if you wish to do so.

Write freely on the questions relative to the different areas of
college life presented in Part II.

Please return your completed questionnaire to the Educational
Records Bureau as soon as possible. A self-addressed, stamped en-
velope is provided for this purpose.

PART I

Please check as many of the following problems as have given you
difficulty. The problems are grouped under four headings. Some
students may find little or nothing in this list to check; others may
find several items that should be checked. Please check all problems
which apply to you, even if this results in more than one check
mark under certain headings. Remember to consider each item to be
checked in relation to the general heading under which it appears.
If you think of other problems that you have found difficult, will you
please enter them under No. 5 and check them.

1. Difficulty in choosing what college to attend
_____ a.   Insufficient secondary school guidance
_____ b.   Insufficient information about colleges

_____ c.   Parental pressure
_____ d.   Lack of clearly defined vocational objectives
_____ e.   Lack of clearly defined educational objectives
_____ f.   Financial needs

2. Difficulty in academic adjustment
_____ g.   Selection of courses for which I am not prepared
_____ h.   Selection of courses in which I have little interest
_____ i.   Lack of experience in taking notes
_____ j.   Large classes
_____ k.   Inability to organize work and study
_____ l.   Questionable teaching ability of instructors
_____ m.   Too much work assigned
_____ n.   High standards of work demanded in college

3. Difficulty in personal adjustment
_____ o.   Lack of success in making friends easily
_____ p.   Feeling of inadequacy in social situations
_____ q.   Worry about conditions at home
_____ r.   Financial worries
_____ s.   Homesickness
_____ t.   Lack of personal attention from the college
_____ u.   Personal health
_____ v.   Lack of, or confusion in, personal objectives in life

4. Group pressures
_____ w.   Overemphasis on extracurricular activities
_____ x.   Hazing
_____ y.   Moral standards of students
_____ z.   Fraternity or sorority influences

5. Other
_____ aa.
_____ bb.
_____ cc.

6. Comment

PART II

Aspects of College Life

This part of the questionnaire is designed to furnish a kind of case history of your adjustment in making the transition from your preparatory school to the freshman year of college. Please discuss each item as fully as you wish. If you need more space, you may write on the back of the page.

1. What comparison would you make between your high school and college work? (*Include such items as instruction or quality of teaching, interest, greatest and least satisfactions, motives for work, strengths and weaknesses of preparation, and so forth. If you feel that certain courses have been especially well taught in college or that others have been taught very poorly, these may be mentioned. Likewise, mention may be made of high school courses that you feel prepared you particularly well for college or courses that you believe contributed little or nothing to your college preparation.*)

2. Write frankly about any significant experiences in adjusting to college, such as being away from home on your own, making friends, influence of roommates, financial problems, conflicting values among classmates, disillusionment concerning college environment, budgeting time, recreation, and so forth. (*Some of these factors may overlap with those elsewhere in the questionnaire.*)

3. This section has to do with the nonacademic life of the college. Comment on each of the following which has any bearing on your group adjustment. Try to point out the chief satisfactions or frustrations that may have resulted from any of the following activities and values or any other aspects of campus life: hazing, fraternities, athletics, parties, religion, moral values, social values, relationship between sexes, multiplicity of activities.

4. To what extent do you think the *college* provides adequate counseling
   (a) about academic problems?
   (b) about personal problems?
   (c) about vocational planning?

5. (a) To what extent have you used any of these services?

   (b) If you have not used the college counseling services, where or to whom have you gone for help if you have had problems you needed to discuss with someone?

6. How could your secondary school have helped you more in anticipating and meeting the adjustment problems of the freshman year?

7. Describe any aspects of your home or community life which you feel have had an important bearing on your adjustment in college.

8. One of the statements which follows is designed to give a rough approximation of your general opinion of your experiences as a freshman in college. (*Check the one with which you are the most nearly in agreement.*)

_____ I have found my freshman year a very satisfactory experience and am enthusiastic about life at this college.

_____ I have found my freshman year generally satisfactory and have no serious criticism to make of the way it is organized and planned.

_____ I have found my freshman year fairly satisfactory, although I believe that in some important ways arrangements for freshmen in this college could be improved significantly.

_____ I have found my freshman year unsatisfactory in several respects which I believe need marked improvement if it is to be a really valuable educational experience.

_____ I have found my freshman year extremely unsatisfactory and feel that I have gained little of value from my experience here.

9. Do you believe that most of your classmates feel as you do about their freshman year, or is your opinion of your experiences unusual among the freshmen of your college?

10. Suggestions for improvement in the college's provisions for freshmen:

11. Before handing in your questionnaire will you please go back to Part I on page 2 and decide whether any changes should be made in your checking of the various items in the light of your answers to the questions in Part II.

List of Participating Colleges

Agricultural and Mechanical College of Texas
Amherst College
Antioch College
Bard College
Bennington College
Brooklyn College
Brown University
Columbia University
Goddard College
Hamilton College
Hunter College of the City of New York
Immaculata College
Lehigh University
University of Louisville
Manhattanville College of the Sacred Heart
Mills College
New Jersey State Teachers College at Trenton
Newton College of the Sacred Heart
Pembroke College of Brown University
University of Pennsylvania
Roanoke College
Sarah Lawrence College
Skidmore College
Wagner Lutheran College
Wesleyan University
University of Wisconsin
Wittenberg College

Index

Guidance—*continued*
  need for help, 22
  philosophy of guidance, 120-21
  reaching the students, 87
  religious counselors, 88
  role of guidance, viii
  roles for the counselor, 82-83
  selection of counselors, 83-84
  self-dependence of students, 92
  self-guidance, 77-78, 80
  specialized services, 85-87
  students as counselors, 89-90
  upperclassmen, 82, 90-91
  value of guidance, 93
  see also Orientation

Harvard, 110
Hazing, 17, 58-59, 68 f., 82
High school:
  anticipating difficulties, 13-14
  college preparation, 36-37, 104
  differences from college, 12-13, 21, 31-33
  English courses, 28-29
  enrichment of the program, 110
  evaluation by freshmen, 26-28
  guidance program, 102, 115-16
  message of freshmen, 114-18
  relationship with colleges, 117-18
  selection of a college, 20-21, 23-24, 26, 119-20
  value of records in college guidance program, 82, 84
Home, 49-50, 78-79
  see also Parents
Honor system, 52

Independence, 18-19, 48-49, 74, 92

Jobs, on campus, 24, 103
  outside the college, 103

Lawrenceville, 110
Library, 12

Maturity, 61-63
Moral values, 19, 62, 69, 78
Motivation, 40-41, 43

Organizing ability, 33
Orientation, 42-43, 102-04, 106-07, 120, 122
  see also Guidance

Parents, 9, 91
  see also Home
Participation, 54
Paternalism, 80
Politics, campus, 55
Portland, Oregon, public schools, 110
Princeton, 110
Program of Early Admission to College, 108

Questionnaire, 4-5, 127-31

Readiness for college, 2-4, 30, 108-09
Reading, 28 ff.
Reed College, 110
Rejection, 56-57
Religion, 88
Residence, 9
  see also Dormitories, Roommates
Responsibility, practice in, 79
Roommates, 17, 45-47
  see also Dormitories, Residence

Set in Linotype Fairfield
Format by Marguerite Swanton
Manufactured by The Haddon Craftsmen, Inc.
Published by HARPER & BROTHERS, New York

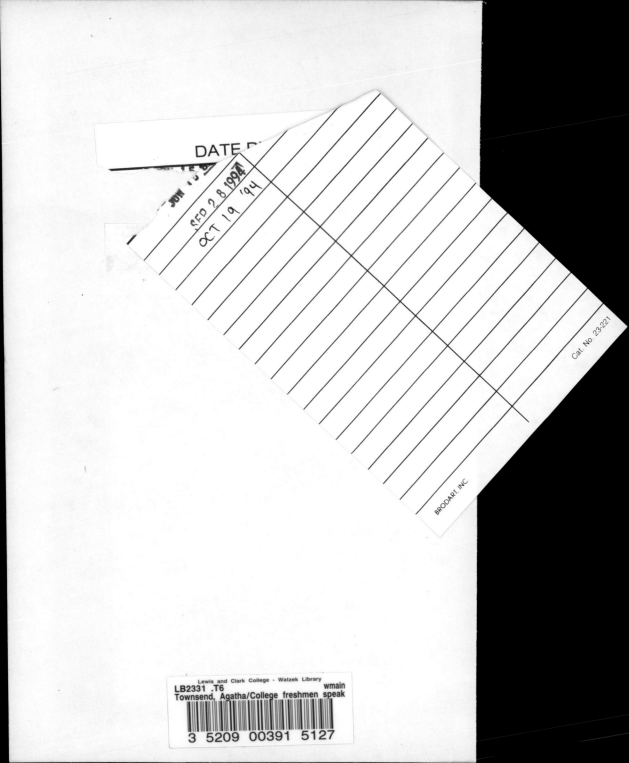